Old English sheepdog puppy, eight weeks old

Toy poodle, apricot, five months old

Long-haired dachshund, red

Ulrich Klever

With 180 Photographs by Monika Wegler Consulting Editor: Matthew M. Vriends, PhD

THE COMPLETE BOOK OF DOG CARE

How to Raise a Happy and Healthy Dog

BARRON'S

Contents

Teaching a Dog to Be a Pleasant Companion 73

Dogs and Their Diet 87

If Your Dog Gets Sick 95

Traveling with a Dog 108

Glossary 112

Breeds: Profiles of Popular Purebred Dogs 130

Great Dane • Doberman Pinscher • Afghan Hound • Saluki • German Shepherd Dog • Collie • Old English Sheepdog (Bobtail) • Chow Chow • Saint Bernard • Boxer • Irish Wolfhound • Irish Setter • Shetland Sheepdog • Golden Retriever • Hovawart • Bernese Mountain Dog • Lhasa Apso • Newfoundland • Kuvasz • Rottweiler • Labrador Retriever • German Spitz • Airedale Terrier • Dalmatian • Schnauzer • Poodle • Cocker Spaniel • Cavalier King Charles Spaniel • Akita • Siberian Husky • Beagle • Bullterrier • Fox Terrier • English Bulldog • French Bulldog • Pug • Basset Hound • Briard • Pyrenean Sheepdog • Dachshund-Basenji • Shih Tzu • West Highland White Terrier • Yorkshire Terrier • Tibetan Terrier • Pekinese • Chihuahua • Miniature Pinscher

Addresses and Literature 167

How to Raise a Healthy, Happy Dog

Preface

The title of this preface expresses the intent of this guide in a nutshell. I have tried to convey to dog owners all they need to know about living with dogs. When a dog joins your household, you have entered a lifelong contract. Its human master becomes for the dog the leader of the pack, and its human family becomes the center of the dog's life. You must be fully aware that entering into a partnership with a dog

- can be almost as demanding as bringing up a child;
- takes time every day;
- costs a considerable amount of money year after year.

You can see that buying a dog is a decision that has to be thought through carefully (see the chapter Dog Ownership without Problems, page 10). Don't buy a dog on impulse, but take time to learn what kind of dog fits in with your personality, habits, and living conditions. You must remember, too, that dogs are runners by nature and consequently need plenty of daily exercise. Just as important is a diet that takes into account canine nutritional needs; dogs are not meant by nature to live off table scraps. Finally, you are taking on the responsibility of maintaining your dog's health, keeping its coat in good condition, and controlling its behavior (see Important Notes, page 175). Topics of special importance for happy coexistence with a dog are covered in the chapter Everyday Life with a Dog, page 27.

In addition to practical advice for daily living, the book also acquaints you with the basic nature of your dog. Dogs are bred by humans and have adjusted to living with humans, but their behavior is still essentially determined by the qualities of their ancestors, the wolves. In the chapters The Dog—An Independent Creature (page 45) and Dogs and Their Behavior (page 54), I try to give you an idea of how dogs perceive their humans and what are the possible consequences of endowing dogs with human traits. This should help you better understand your dog and its reactions. You also learn about the vocal and body language of dogs, which will help you respond properly to your dog's behavior. This is important for a happy life together, for only someone who understands the behavior of dogs can train them with firmness and handle them with confidence. Because I know from my own experience how much depends on the training of a dog, I have devoted an extensive chapter to this topic (Teaching a Dog to Become a Pleasant Companion, page 73).

The sum of my varied experience has gone into this book—both the practical experience I have gained in the course of living with dogs and the more theoretical knowledge that I have acquired as a zoologist and author of many successful books on dogs. I hope this guide will help you create a happy bond with a healthy, obedient dog, perhaps even to form a friendship that at its profoundest moments has need of neither words nor outward signs.

Ulrich Klever

Opposite page: For children as for dogs, playing is half the fun of life. In the picture: A boy and his mixed breed Yorkshire terrier.

Dog Ownership without Problems

When a dog joins your household you should be undertaking a contract for the life of the dog. You are becoming the dog's family, for dogs by nature live in packs and need contact with other dogs. In the course of time dogs have learned to modify their need to live only with creatures of their own kind and to accept humans as substitutes: Dog has become our "best friend." To break the bond between a human being and a dog is tragic for the dog. That is why it is so important to remember that *a partnership with a dog*

- will probably last about 10 years;
- will cost you a significant amount of money every year;
- can be as much trouble as a child;
- will take two to three hours every day;
- presupposes that you have enough room to house the animal properly and to allow for enough exercise.

Only if you are willing to meet these conditions should you consider sharing your life with a dog.

I strongly advise against *buying a dog on impulse*. Never acquire a dog out of pity, because "it looks so cute," because it's the thing to do, or—least of all—as a surprise for the family. The purchase of a dog has to be carefully considered and discussed, if possible, by the whole family.

Anyone planning to get a dog should have a feeling for animals in general and for dogs in particular. Otherwise the purchase may lead to a scene like this:

The "Vicious" Scottie

A Scottie puppy (Scottish terrier) was sold to a woman who had never had a dog before and who probably didn't have great rapport with animals. She didn't know that hunting dogs—and consequently her Scottie—try to nip people's heels in play because they are used to doing it to their mothers. The woman ran off screaming, the dog after her in hot pursuit, squealing with delight. The 12-week-old puppy was then accused of trying to attack its owner.

The Scottie was bought back by the breeder. Now almost one year old, the Scottie is a completely normal dog that has long since lost interest in nipping anyone's heels. If he had stayed with the uninformed purchaser, he might well be a habitual biter by now. The short-term owner of the Scottie, on the other hand, probably tells people to watch out for vicious Scottish terriers.

Questions before the Purchase

If you are thinking about buying a dog for the first time, you are faced with a number of questions. To help prevent problems, I will answer these questions in this chapter. My many years of experience and study enable me to offer useful information. You will notice that I generally recommend one course of action and avoid suggesting alternatives. This practice grows out of my close dealings with dogs, from which I have learned that dogs demand authority. My clear-cut advice will also make life with a dog simpler for you.

Where Should You Buy a Dog?

Since the various members of a family often have quite different conceptions of the "ideal dog," the purchase should be discussed at length and by everybody. Even when the time comes to pick up the dog, both the husband and the wife, as well as older children, should be involved. This is especially important if you are getting a grown dog from an animal shelter (see page 12). Such a dog often forms a spontaneous attachment to the person who picks it up and may only reluctantly let other members of the family approach.

You can get a dog:

At pet stores (see page 11).

From a kennel. Addresses of kennels are available from the American Kennel Club (see Addresses, page 167).

From hobby breeders and dog owners who have planned as well as unplanned puppies for sale. These people often advertise in local newspapers. Look in the classified ad section "Animals."

From your local animal shelter.

A Puppy or a Grown Dog?

The younger the dog, the more it will become *your* dog and the more influence you will have on shaping its character. Young here means 10 to 12 weeks old. It is very important to pick up your dog yourself (see page 79). This may be inconvenient, but the positive effects will last for the dog's life. Being shipped—no matter by what method—means being isolated in a container; this is such a shocking experience for a puppy that there is no telling how its psyche may be affected even much later (see page 12).

A **puppy** requires a great deal of attention during the first six months, and you shouldn't take a vacation from it during this period. Puppies are much like small children: They want to be part of everything; they want to know how they fit in; they want a regular routine; and they want someone to do things with. This last is very impor-

tant. The more you teach a young puppy, the easier life together will be later on. Make the most of these early days, for a day in a puppy's life is like a week or even a month in ours. Dogs live faster and consequently pack more experience into a brief period. They will never again be as eager to learn as they are when they are very young (see Teaching a Dog to Become a Pleasant Companion, page 73).

Getting a **grown dog** seems at first glance much less complicated.

- It is already housebroken.
- It is more or less trained and past the stage of youthful rambunctiousness.

So far so good. But remember: A grown dog comes with a fully formed personality, including good and bad traits. Now it has to learn to understand you, a totally unfamiliar human, and adjust to your ways. You have to help in this process. This takes lots of patience and understanding, especially if you have no "instruction manual" from the dog's former owner. For this reason I recommend fully grown dogs only to older people with some experience in dealing with dogs.

Should You Buy Dogs from Pet Stores?

Yes, if you purchase the puppy from a reputable pet dealer or from the pet department of a large department store. The majority of these puppies come from serious breeding establishments, are properly vaccinated, and have the necessary papers that are proof of their descent.

No, if the above conditions are not met. Nor should you buy a dog from animal dealers (breeders) who, using the guise of a kennel name, sell dozens of breeds.

Getting a Dog from a Kennel

If you get a puppy from a properly run kennel you can pick out the exact animal you want. You can get to know its mother, and the kennel owner will also point out the father to you. You can see the world in which the puppy has been growing up, and the breeder can give you detailed background on the typical traits of the breed and the individual characteristics of your particular puppy. This gives you a better picture of how your dog will look and act later on. You can discuss if and how the puppy has been wormed and vaccinated (see page 98). The breeder will also tell you how to handle the dog properly, and you can always later ask for advice. A conscientious kennel owner may even dissuade you from buying a dog there if the breed is not appropriate for you.

You will recognize *a good kennel owner* with good dogs instantly when you visit. The puppies don't spend all their time in cages; instead they are brought up in the house, where they have contact with humans. This contact should be established during the first few weeks of life. A good kennel owner will deliver to you a physically and emotionally healthy dog with all the proper documents. Among these are: the vaccination record (see page 99) and the registration paper with the date of the litter's birth and confirmation of entry into the breed's register.

If you buy a puppy from a hobby breeder you can also see the environment it grew up in and who its parents are—except, of course, if you choose a mongrel; in that case you at least get to see the puppy's mother.

Buying through the Mail?

Dogs young enough for events to leave an indelible mark and affect their future personality should not be shipped like merchandise. The shock of being shipped leaves a psychic scar and can lead to behavioral problems later (see page 101). You don't choose your car from a catalog, so you shouldn't even consider this method of acquiring a companion that will be with you for ten years or so. It's true that the immediate availability of dogs sold through the mail can be tempting. You order, and almost immediately you get a dog of the desired breed, when you might have to wait several months if you purchase a puppy from a kennel. But I can only warn you: Mail-order dogs almost always come from mass operations, the puppy mills, where dogs are bred and kept in cages like pigs. These operations are run not by breeders dedicated to a particular breed, but by entrepreneurs interested in profit.

It is *typical for the mail-order trade in dogs* that a number of popular breeds are offered for sale, among them currently fashionable ones, like West Highland White terriers and Yorkshire terriers, as well as all-time favorites like cocker spaniels. These dogs are almost always sick and emotionally unstable, and if they survive at all you will end up spending on veterinarian's bills many times more than what you originally paid for the dog. Please do what you can—it's in your own interest—to end this exploitive business by not buying your dog by mail order.

A Dog from an Animal Shelter?

This route can be recommended only with reservations, because it is always a bit of a gamble. You know nothing—or very little—about the dog's previous life (unless the staff at the shelter can give you some information), and in the case of a mongrel puppy you never know how it will look and act when full grown. Don't count on getting a well-behaved, reliably housebroken, unproblematic dog. You are safest if you pick a purebred puppy at the shelter.

On the other hand, every dog that is adopted from a shelter means a dog life saved. In shelters you find only unwanted dogs that are there as a result of a death or sickness in the family, divorce, or a move to rented quarters where pets are not allowed. Or they may be animals that were taken there or abandoned because their owners got tired of them. Older dogs are the most pitiful because hardly anyone wants them. These may be problem animals, but they *can* also turn out to be a perfect match.

Male or Female?

I can't give you definite advice here, because a dog's sex is a matter of personal preference. Forget all the generalizations you may have heard, such as: Female dogs are more affectionate, or: Male dogs get attached only to the man in the family. Every dog is different.

But two things are beyond debate:

- Female dogs come into heat twice a year and can get pregnant at these times (see Glossary, ESTRUS).
- Male dogs constantly display their amorousness when there is a female in heat in the neighborhood. They lift their legs more often than usual on walks to leave scent marks (see page 66).

Here is my advice: Conduct an informal survey about how many male and female dogs live in your neighborhood, and then follow the example of the majority of dog owners. This will make your life easier.

Note: It is not true, by the way, that every female dog should be allowed to have puppies at least once.

Does It Have to Be a Purebred Dog?

Purebred dogs have specific, well-developed traits and talents. This is not the case with mongrels, which are mixtures of several breeds. At present, dogs of mixed breeds seem to be in favor with the public. It is often true that mutts are more intelligent and more stable than highly bred dogs produced to embody external perfection. On the other hand, the owner of a purebred dog has a fairly accurate idea of what to expect from the dog. Also, mongrels may often be smarter, healthier, and less neurotic than purebreds, but they are not necessarily so. In mixed breeding, too, much depends on parentage, which is often unknown. That is why getting a mongrel always involves an element of chance. You may hit the jackpot, but then again you may not.

The Big Question: Which Breed?

Anyone involved with dogs has a picture of the dog of one's dreams. Often, however, the breed of this dog doesn't fit the realities of one's life—perhaps it is too large, too expensive, too difficult to keep. You simply have to accept your limitations. You should not experiment with a questionable choice. It is of course wonderful if your

Mixed breeds, too, make beautiful and lovable pets. In this picture the dog on the left is primarily a short-haired fox terrier and the one on the right is a mixture of hunting breeds.

13

dream dog does fit in with your life. Happily, there is much to choose from: There are over 300 different breeds. From these I have picked 47 of the most popular ones, which I introduce in this book, complete with photos (see Breeds, pages 128-166).

Purebred dogs result from breeding only members of a recognized breed of unmixed ancestry. Appearance and certain traits therefore remain constant from generation to generation.

The registration papers of a purebred dog (see Glossary, REGISTRATION PAPERS) are proof that the dog is in fact purebred.

The purity of the breed is maintained through strict supervision of breeding according to rules (see Glossary, PUREBRED). The dogs themselves are not the least bit concerned with these rules, which is why the world is full of mongrels.

The breed character is the sum of a breed's distinguishing qualities and traits.

But beyond the qualities of its breed, each dog has its own unique personality that matters more than anything else when you live with a dog. Personality is more important than physical beauty or the most impressive pedigree.

To sum up: Make a conscientious effort to find a breed that truly matches your desires and situation. In the section on the different breeds you will discover their various needs and qualities.

Dog and Cat?

Cats and dogs can get along, as I found from my own experience, as long as

- there is room for the animals to avoid each other if they wish;
- the dog belongs to a breed that is not aggressive and the cat is friendly.

The best way is to get a young kitten if you have a grown dog or to let a puppy and a kitten grow up together. It is harder to introduce a dog into a household that has previously included cats only.

Following its natural inclinations, a dog will regard *other pets* like hamsters, guinea pigs, or rabbits as legitimate prey. You either have to keep the two types of animals strictly segregated, or do without one or the other. The fact that unlikely friendships do sometimes develop between vastly different animals is the proverbial exception to the rule. Since birds are usually kept in cages and are not the natural prey of most dogs, dogs and birds don't usually bother each other.

A Second Dog

The prerequisite for getting a second dog is that there be enough space—preferably a yard and several rooms—for each dog to have a retreat when it wants peace and quiet. If the second dog is a puppy, the adjustment is usually smooth. If the newcomer is already fully grown, you have to proceed with more caution and, above all: Don't try to force anything.

An ideal combination is a male and a spayed female.

Trickier are two bitches, because they often don't get along.

Difficult: Two males, because sooner or later there will be fights to establish dominance. Once the *rank order* has been established (see page 59), coexistence presents no further complications. It is important, however, that the dogs be treated with absolute evenhandedness.

What cannot be foreseen is whether both dogs will fit into the family harmoniously or whether they will form a pack of their own within the human family.

An Eight-legged Friendship

This is a personal story. When our basset hound Henry was eight years old we got a second basset, five-month-old David. At first things looked anything but rosy. For six months Henry treated David as though he didn't exist. Invitations to play were met at best with ill-humored growls. We were on the point of accepting our failure; we would have to live with two dogs that refused to speak to each other.

Luckily our house and yard are large enough that everyone could have managed. Then one day, I don't know why or how, the two were running circles together in the yard. The young dog was trying to catch the old one, and the old one let himself be chased. From that moment on the two were the best of friends, and our

sedate Henry acted years younger and livelier under the influence of his new playmate. When David was three years old, he tried several times to challenge Henry's rank and to become boss himself. We didn't have the heart to let them fight it out, and so rank based on age continued. We were disappointed only in one respect: When the two were left alone, they refused to be consoled by each other's company; instead they bemoaned their misery together, setting up a communal, very loud chorus of howls.

Dog and Baby— Can It Work?

If the dog is already part of the family when the baby arrives, it will accept the new member as part of the pack. Not only that; it will regard the baby as a new puppy that has to be put up with and protected. Unhappy experiences are very rare (they occur only with highly neurotic dogs), and stories recounting them are usually distorted. If you don't neglect the dog on account of the baby and don't give it any reason to become jealous, everyone will get along. If the dog bites a stranger who is picking up the baby, it is acting out of its instinct to protect the young of the pack.

Growing up together is a wonderful experience for both the child and the dog: Both profit and learn from each other (see Dogs for children, pages 40–42).

When a baby is on the way, you should have your dog examined by the veterinarian and tell your own doctor that you have a dog. You should also be especially careful about hygiene (see page 103). Once the baby is born, the dog is not a source of infection for the child. Recent medical findings have established that when humans and animals live together, their bacterial flora become similar. What this means is that children develop an immunity to many pathogens. All the same, make sure that small children and dogs

• don't eat out of the same dishes;
• don't lick each other;
• don't sleep in the same bed.

If you teach a dog ahead of time not to enter the room that will be the baby's, it will keep out of it later on.

Double spread on following pages: An Old English sheepdog playing with a ball.

Necessary Basic Equipment

I always say that just purchasing a dog doesn't automatically make you into the dog's master. This status can be achieved only through concerned living with the animal. Well, let's get started! When your dog first arrives, it is still a "poor" dog, for it has nothing except its owner. But to feel at ease in your home and to live in a civilized manner, a dog needs a number of things.

A Dog Needs a Name

The first thing a puppy needs is a name. The one it is given at the kennel and that is entered in its papers might not be suitable for everyday use, because the names of all the puppies of a litter have the same initial. This sometimes leads to strange-sounding names (see Glossary, NAMING DOGS). Since you will and should say the dog's name frequently, it should be a word that is easy to understand and doesn't sound harsh like a command or a rebuke. Two-syllable words with the vowels a, o, or u are especially good. Donna, Pola, Numa, and Bosco are some examples. If you choose to call your dog Otto, be prepared that not everybody named Otto will be amused. Remember, too, that you may occasionally have to call your dog in a crowd. I don't know how comfortable you will feel shouting something like "Pocahontas," which seemed like such a clever name when you chose it. Still, don't be afraid to use your imagination when naming your dog. If I were a dog and my people called me Champ or Cato or Foxy or Waldo, that would suit me just fine.

Of all the things a dog should have, the following are absolutely essential:
- a bed
- a blanket
- two bowls
- a collar
- a leash
- a brush or a comb

Dog accessories like these are available at pet supply stores, or they can be ordered through specialty catalogs. You will find addresses of mail-order businesses in dog magazines.

A Bed

Every dog needs a place to which it can retire and that is always reserved for it. This can be a mattress, an open or cavelike basket, a box, or a thick pad. The dog's bed serves primarily to keep the animal off the cold floor. Whatever kind of bed you choose, it should be large enough for the dog to stretch out, even though dogs usually sleep rolled up in a ball. To be sure it will be large enough, measure a fully grown dog of the breed you have from the tip of its nose to the tip of the tail. If you buy a bed to fit the puppy, you'll have to buy a bigger one nine months later.

Note: Wicker baskets are not recommended for young dogs that are still at the nibbling and chewing stage, and cavelike baskets are available only for small dogs.

An Easy-care Blanket

You have to be able to wash and disinfect a dog's blanket easily, because it may become infested with fleas. An old woolen blanket is a cheap solution (and quite adequate for the beginning), but better yet is a special dog blanket that not only warms and is soft, but also helps keep the dog dry. Your dealer can show you several brands, including the "Dognapper," for instance. This is not a cheap blanket, but it is of excellent quality. You can even in a pinch use it directly on the floor of a terrace or balcony, because it insulates so well.

Two Bowls, for the Dog Only

Each dog should have its own bowls—one for food, the other for water, because fresh water must always be available. Over the years we have come to prefer
- a heavy water bowl made of glazed stoneware;
- an enameled food bowl made of solid

metal and placed on a nubbly rubber mat where it cannot slide;

- stainless steel bowls are also good. What matters is that
- the bowls be heavy so the dog cannot play with them;
- they have a slip-proof bottom or are placed on a slip-proof mat. A mat has the added advantage that it keeps the floor from getting messy.
- The bowls should be easy to clean.
- For dogs with long lop ears there are special, cone-shaped bowls that narrow toward the top and keep the ears from drooping into the food and water. There are also practical small stands with places for both bowls next to each other.

The Collar

A puppy's first collar can be very plain, because it will soon be outgrown. A collar has two functions:
- It allows you to hold the dog securely either with your hand or with a leash.
- It can adorn the dog.

This means that the collar should, first of all, be strong enough to withstand the pulling force of the dog and, secondly, that its style be in keeping with the dog's breed and appeal to our sense of beauty. Above all, it should be well-made.

The variety of collars is so great that it is confusing. Most have buckles, which in itself presents a problem. If the collar is set too loose, the dog can slip its head out of it and get off the leash; if it is too tight, the dog is uncomfortable. All this can be avoided if you get

- *a choke collar* that tightens as needed. But be sure to buy one with a stop that allows the ring to move only to a certain point. If there is no such stop, you could choke your dog to death or the dog might strangle itself on the collar.
- *a harness* that is worn loosely around the neck and chest. These harnesses look attractive, but they are suitable only for dogs that don't pull too hard. I'm not speaking here of the special harnesses designed for sled dogs.

A chain or a leather collar? Chain

If a small child and a dog are growing up together, it is important to maintain good hygiene, but there is no need to worry. The picture shows a child with a seven-week-old Eurasier puppy.

collars are especially convenient because you can carry a second one in your pocket (important for training walks, see page 81), but the metal does discolor light fur. Most dog owners use leather collars.

A collar should be the right style for the dog. A German shepherd dog in a rhinestone collar looks ridiculous, as does a dachshund with a heavy metal collar. There are special collars with badger hair ruffs designed for bull terriers, French bulldogs, and mastiffs; for Swiss mountain dogs there are collars with cow-shaped brass ornaments. But don't buy an expensive collar until your dog has reached its full size.

The Leash

Whether you buy a short or a long leash depends on personal preference and the size of the dog.

A leash with an automatic rewind mechanism and about 15 feet (5 m) long can serve as both a short and a long leash. There is a lock you can operate with your thumb that lets you set the length. With this you can give the dog a controllable radius of movement or keep it on a very short leash for heeling. The disadvantage is that you have to hold on to a rather large plastic box with a handle. If you drop it, the rewinding mechanism makes the box clatter toward the dog, who is bound to be startled and may bolt. It's up to the dog's owner to decide on the width, material,

A small sampling of leashes and collars. The choke collar with the spurs should be used only with an extremely obstinate dog

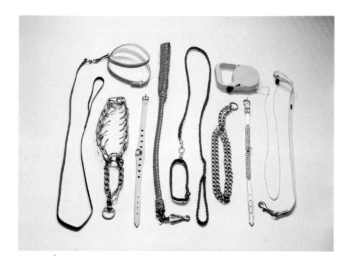

and style of the leash, again taking into account the breed of the dog.

Important: The clip that links the leash to the collar has to hold securely. There are three types of clips:
- *A simple spring clip* is quite secure, but the leash can be taken off the collar only by exerting considerable pressure with the thumb.
- *A scissor-type clip* can be opened more quickly and easily, but as the spring gets weaker, it may occasionally open by itself.
- *A clip with a safety catch* (my personal choice) is easy to open with one hand and will stay attached to the collar even if the spring breaks.

Brush, Comb, and Currycomb

A brush is essential for any dog, no matter what its breed, and every dog loves being brushed properly.

For short-haired breeds you should get
- a coarse brush of natural bristles for a first rough brushing;
- a currycomb of soft plastic or rubber for removing by static electricity the hairs loosened by the first brushing;
- a chamois cloth to shine up the coat after the cleaning.

For long-haired dogs, the procedure is more complicated, and you need
- a normal hairbrush with a strong handle, particularly if the dog is still a puppy and its coat is not yet very thick. Since the puppy will regard the brush as a toy rather than as a tool and will chew on it, it will probably not last longer than a few months. Then you will need
- a coarse-toothed comb;
- a fine-toothed comb;
- a wire brush with rounded corners—so that they will not injure the skin—and with bristles mounted on an elastic rubber cushion;
- a brush made of stiff natural bristles.
I'm opposed to using brushes with artificial bristles because they seem to me too hard and scratchy. The breeder

from whom you are buying your puppy will show you the best tools to use with the breed in question.

What Else You Need

In addition to the basic essentials there are a few other accessories that are very useful.

For car travel:

- *a protective net (or grate)* that separates the back of the car from the front, keeps the dog from climbing or jumping into the front seat, and restrains it if you have to brake suddenly;
- *a special kind of cover* that can be stretched over the back seat and makes a safe, tub-like space for the dog;
- *a screen* that can be clamped into a partially open car window and allows air to enter but keeps strangers from reaching in and prevents the dog from sticking its head out of the window (see page 111).

A dog whistle is needed if you go somewhere where you can let your dog roam but want to be able to call it back from some distance. The whistle is also useful in the training that is necessary before the dog can be allowed to go off so far. A dog whistle always has the same authoritative sound to the dog, and it carries farther than your voice. I strongly recommend using an ultrasonic whistle, whose sound is inaudible to human ears (see page 49). This way you can avoid disturbing other people with shrill whistling.

Waterproof paper bags and cardboard scrapers or clean-up kits are needed to pick up dog feces. Depending on where you live, you may need to take this equipment along when you take your dog out.

A muzzle, which usually consists of an arrangement of leather strips, is placed over a dog's face to keep it from biting. The muzzle has to fit well, be comfortable, and not slip out of place. Muzzles are obligatory for dogs that bite—even during visits to the veterinarian. Muzzles are also necessary in rabies districts if a dog has not had rabies shots, and in cities and countries that have legislation requiring the use of muzzles. It is the owner's responsibility to know the relevant law.

An outdoor shelter for occasional housing is very useful for large, hardy breeds like herding dogs, Saint Bernards, and Newfoundlands, or excitable watchdogs like Dobermans, Rottweilers, and bullterriers. Examine the shelters at the kennel where you are buying your dog, or get catalogs from mail-order houses that

Picture on left: Dog toys should not be made of plastic or soft rubber and should be too large to be swallowed.

Picture on right: Essential items for grooming: a coarse-toothed comb, a brush, and a currycomb.

advertise in dog magazines like *Dog World*, P.O. Box 6500, Chicago, IL 60680. There are also indoor and travel cages that keep dogs out of trouble in the car or in a hotel.

Dog toys should always be made of a suitable material that is not harmful to the dog, and they should not be small enough to be swallowed. Toys made of plastic or soft rubber should be avoided, and toys in the shape of cats are in bad taste. A rawhide bone is an excellent toy that allows a growing dog to exercise its teeth and chewing muscles. Solid rubber balls (where there is nothing to bite off) are also acceptable.

Dog clothing of any sort, from sweaters to coats to booties, is unnecessary. A dog's coat is such an efficient all-weather protection that any textile manufacturer would be only too happy to obtain the production formula.

Exceptions: Older dogs, hairless breeds, or small and delicate short-hairs like Chihuahuas or miniature pinschers may occasionally wear a sweater for warmth. But keep in mind that pampered dogs are less hardy and get sick more easily.

Intimate apparel: Putting panties on a dog during heat may look grotesque, but it does keep blood spots from floors.

What about sleepwear if your dog sleeps in your bed? That is a question I leave up to your own sense of hygiene. My personal feelings are that if a dog is allowed into bed, then it should be without pajamas because they surely interfere with the dog's comfort.

Wastl in Bavarian Folk Costume

Wastl, a wirehaired dachshund, was not a particularly robust dog, but he was unmistakably a dachshund. Unfortunately he looked like a caricature of himself, because he almost always had on a gray jacket decorated with green appliqué oak leaves, and when it got cold, he wore a wool coat. His clothes were a replica of the Bavarian folk costume, for he lived in Bavaria. His owner was very proud of his

clothes because she had sewn and knitted them herself. The problem was Wastl's fur, which was getting thinner and thinner. The veterinarian blamed this on the clothes, so the owner changed veterinarians. Then one day a hunting dog grabbed Wastl by his back and shook him. The jacket kept Wastl from getting seriously hurt, but it was also the cause of the incident. It had been raining, and the jacket smelled like rabbit, as the new veterinarian determined later. That is why the hunting dog had gone after Wastl.

Wastl no longer wears his Bavarian costume, and his fur is already getting thicker.

If neatness matters to you and you like to have all your dog's utensils in one place, you may want to build or buy a small cabinet or clear a large drawer to store dog-related items. This will save your wasting time looking for them later.

Don't Forget the Costs

"The necessary small change": By this I don't mean the change you put into a small pocket on the collar so that the dog's finder can call you if your dog should run off sometime. I mean the costs involved in keeping a dog. For dogs are more costly to keep than any other household pet.

The purchase: It doesn't matter whether you are given a puppy, whether you get one for a few ten-dollar bills at a shelter, or whether you pay a considerable sum for a purebred dog; compared to the money you will spend over the dog's lifetime, the purchase price is of minor consequence. That is why you should not pinch pennies when buying a dog. The cheaper dog always ends up costing more money in the long run. Veterinarian's bills may add up to several times the purchase price if you have fallen for "a special." Dogs bought from a breeder are expensive, but no breeder gets rich selling dogs. Dogs bought through the mail may be cheaper, but someone is still making a

profit. Don't try to bargain when buying a dog; it's not worth it.

Accessories: Depending on how much you buy, what quality you choose, and how often you replace things, you may end up spending quite a bit of money on accessories and supplies. Outfitting a dog can come to about $100 a year.

Food: It's the ongoing costs that add up. A dog has to eat every day, and it needs its own special food. Depending on the dog's size and breed and on whether you prepare its food yourself, whether you buy the ingredients at the butcher's or the supermarket, or whether you use commercial dog food, you will spend between one and three dollars a day. That adds up to between $365 and $1,095 a year. Over a period of ten years that is a considerable outlay.

License fees: Fees vary with the size of the community and from region to region. Currently they generally range from $20 to $100 per year (see Glossary, LICENSE FEES).

Insurance: You should not try to save by doing without liability insurance for your dog, because if you do you may have to pay dearly at some point. You have to figure on $50 to $75 (see Glossary, LIABILITY INSURANCE.)

Veterinarian's bills: You'll have to take your dog to the vet's at least once a year for shots, and additional visits may be necessary if the dog gets sick or hurt. I budget $200 per year but always end up spending more.

Dog parlor: If you have a dog that has to be shorn or clipped, this is an additional expense. Whether you take it to the "beauty salon" every six weeks or only a couple of times a year, you should figure on about $100 a year.

Dog clubs: If you join a dog club, the annual dues will be about $25.

If you add up all these numbers and, for simplicity's sake, figure on a life span of ten years, you'll find that you are taking on a financial obligation of about $6,000 to $12,000 when you decide to get a dog. Sound frightening? Try adding up what a car costs you over the same period of time.

There are certain obligations that go along with having a purebred dog. Figure on paying more for the dog initially and on membership fees for the dog club. Shown is a Dalmatian with its eight-week-old puppy.

Legal Questions Relating to Dog Ownership

A Dog in a Rented Apartment

Before you buy a puppy you should read your lease very carefully. Are you allowed to keep a dog in your apartment at all? On the whole, legal opinion is best expressed by the phrase "well-mannered dogs permitted." Community life depends on mutual consideration, and a dog lover living in an apartment house may expect that others will accept the dog owner's feelings for animals. In return, one must respect a neighbor's need for quiet and expectations of cleanliness. A dog owner should discuss these matters with the landlord and/or neighbors before buying a dog.

The legal situation: There is among our many laws unfortunately none that stands as a clear-cut legal statement regarding the right to keep dogs in rented apartments. Our civil rights imply the right to express our personalities without constraint, which would seem to include owning a dog with reasonable manners. This *may* be true even if, according to the lease, the landlord's permission is required for keeping pets. Thus, should this be upheld, the plaintiff would have to establish that the dog in question represents an unacceptable nuisance to other tenants (by, for example, making too much noise or creating unsanitary conditions) even if there is a clause in the lease that pets are not allowed.

At this time, however, I urge you to reach an agreement with your landlord and/or not to sign a lease that prohibits pets. There is only one thing I consider worse than not being able to get a dog, and that is to have to get rid of one simply because you are moving. No one should ever consider doing that to a pet.

Note: It is always advisable to consult your local tenants' association or some other body representing tenants' rights.

A Dog in Your Own Home

Here you don't have to ask anyone's permission to keep dogs. In row houses, however, particularly if there are no fences, it is wise to have some kind of agreement with the neighbors and to make sure that the dog does not bother them. If you have trained your dog properly and are considerate of others, you will save yourself a lot of unpleasantness.

Your Dog and Your Neighbors

If a dog is kept in an apartment or a row house, it lives a partly public life. The neighbors hear it, meet it on the stairs, see it in the streets, and come across its feces.

A dog is appreciated by others if it

- obeys its master's commands instantly;
- doesn't bark at the slightest noise;
- doesn't bark at or jump up on strangers;
- doesn't relieve itself in the middle of the sidewalk.

A Dog and Its Excrements

The problem of dog feces is primarily a question of how considerate we are of others. The greatest objection people have to having dogs around arises from this problem. Here I shall once more have to resort to "legal talk." Dogs should not relieve themselves on the sidewalk, but, as every dog owner knows, it sometimes cannot be avoided. The owner is fined because the law recognizes a potential danger to public health if dogs relieve themselves on public sidewalks. The decision is based on the medical fact that certain diseases can be transmitted to humans by dogs. In addition, dog feces on sidewalks present another danger, namely, they can cause pedestrians to slip and get hurt.

To keep dogs from urinating against doors, the corners of the doors should be sprayed with a substance whose smell

Opposite page: The largest and the smallest dogs: A Chihuahua is sitting between the front feet of an Irish wolfhound.

Dogs and cats can live together happily if each has enough room of its own. In the picture a Yorkshire terrier, its four-month-old puppy, and a Persian cat are posing together.

offends a dog's nose. The same kind of substance can be used to spray chair legs and other tempting or vulnerable pieces of furniture.

There are also various clean-up products available in your pet store. These are designed to inhibit and destroy dog smell by eliminating the bacteria that produce it. A practical household remedy that can be used in an emergency is a solution of vinegar and water. This is quite effective in eliminating the characteristic odor of ammonia that develops in an area that has been doused with urine. After letting the vinegar solution soak in for several minutes blot thoroughly with paper towels. Scrubbing with a mild detergent solution and blotting with paper towels is moderately effective, especially if you finish off with a vinegar spray. (Use 50 percent vinegar and 50 percent water in a pump spray like those designed for misting plants.)

Everyday Life with a Dog

Your dog has arrived. Everything necessary has been bought. Now begins the reality of daily living with your dog. Dogs are creatures that require authority. Happiest if their lives are ruled by rigid routine, they strongly dislike changes, and want to know exactly how they fit into the scheme of things. You will have to organize your life accordingly. Remember that you have promised yourself to help your dog be physically, emotionally, and socially comfortable. I understand this to mean that the dog should be allowed to live in tune with its own needs and that you will respect its inborn qualities and behavior. Part of this is establishing certain places as the dog's own and setting up definite routines, for dogs are by nature creatures of habit.

Eating Place and Sleeping Corner

The Eating Place

The bowls you've bought for your dog should have a permanent place. That is where the dog is always fed, preferably at the same time every day. The kitchen is probably the best place because the kitchen floor is usually easy to clean. Dogs tend to spill their food, especially if they are the kind that shakes every bite before eating it. Put the dishes in a corner if you can, or at least in an out-of-the-way spot, never where there is much traffic. Dogs don't like to be disturbed while they are eating. If a dog is interrupted too often during its meals

- it may start wolfing down its food;
- or the opposite: it becomes a reluctant eater;
- or it may think that people are trying to steal its food.

Then it may start defending the food so that nobody can enter the kitchen while the dog is eating. This behavior is difficult to cure, but if you choose the food place with care you can prevent the problem.

The water bowl can be placed next to the food dish, or somewhere else, as in the hallway or (a second bowl, perhaps) next to the bed. It should always be full of fresh water. I don't subscribe to the theory that dogs should be given water only when they are thirsty lest drinking too much water make their muscles slack. If a dog drinks unusually much, it may be for one of the following reasons:

- The dog needs a lot of liquid because it is fed dry dog food.
- The dog is sick, in which case it should be taken to the veterinarian to determine what is wrong.
- Your dog is drinking out of boredom. If this is the case, you should control its drinking and also spend more time with the animal.

The Sleeping Corner

The dog's bed—the spot where it sleeps at night and rests during the day—also should be in a quiet corner and away from drafts. If you live in an apartment, the bed should not be in the hallway or next to the

be a blanket to keep the dog off the cold floor.

At night dogs love best sleeping in a bedroom. There are understandable reasons for this. Conditioned by its ancestral wolf past, a dog always wants to be close to its humans and feels banished if locked out of the bedroom. This is not true if you have two or more dogs. They can form a pack of their own and sleep together somewhere else. To let one of several dogs sleep in the bedroom is wrong: This dog would feel so favored that the whole dog hierarchy would be upset.

It is *absolutely essential* that a dog whose owners work and are away from home all day be allowed to sleep with its humans. Such a dog's bed belongs in the bedroom. The compromise solution of separate bedrooms if one half of a couple refuses to sleep with a dog in the room leads to the dog's becoming much more attached to the person in whose bedroom it sleeps. Keep in mind, after all, that the night is the longest stretch of time the dog spends close to its people. Closeness here means physical proximity but not necessarily physical contact.

A dog in the bed. Most dog owners deny that their pets sleep with them, but the real picture is somewhat different. I read the following figures in a recent survey: Forty percent of the dog owners let their dogs get on the bed (only the foot end, of course!); 20 percent would like to share their beds with the dog but don't for hygienic reasons; and the rest find the idea of dogs on beds disgusting. It's all a matter of opinion.

If basic hygiene is observed and the dog has had all necessary vaccinations, there is very little danger of transmission of canine diseases to humans.

The danger of infection increases rapidly, however, if the rooms and the dishes used by dogs are not cleaned regularly and carefully (see page 103).

My personal view: I am in favor of letting a dog in the bedroom if it sleeps on its own chair or mattress. But I don't like dogs on my bed; it's too uncomfortable. I also object to a dog basket in the bedroom because, first of all, a basket is hard to

Picture above: Even if two dogs get along they should not permanently have to share one dish.

Picture below: A classic dog basket in which a dog can curl up comfortably. The dog in this particular basket is a dachshund.

door, where the dog may assume the role of watchdog for the entire building. A dog spends not only the night but also much daytime in its bed, unless it has taken to lying on a soft armchair, for dogs prefer not to lie at floor level. To keep your dog from taking over all the chairs you can give it its own. Put the dog's blanket on one chair, less to protect the upholstery than to make the dog feel that this chair belongs to it.

If you live in a house with a yard, the dog's daytime resting place can be near the door. After all, you want your dog to let you know when strangers approach.

In the summer dogs love to lie outside the door or on a balcony, where they can nap or watch the world. But there should

keep clean and, secondly, because it creaks if the dog moves during the night.

I put a second water bowl next to the bedroom door in case the dog gets thirsty at night. The occasional nocturnal lapping of water doesn't bother me.

Fluffy and Grandmother's Bed

Fluffy is a beagle who is allowed to sleep on his owner's bed. When the family went away on a trip, Grandmother agreed to look after the house and Fluffy. She let him sleep in the guest bedroom with her but refused to have him up on the bed. Grandmother remained firm in spite of Fluffy's whining and begging, and she threw him off the bed when he jumped up on her feet. The second night he scratched at the door. He evidently needed to go out. Grandmother got up and put on her bathrobe. As she walked toward the door, Fluffy dashed past her, leaped into the empty bed, snuggled up against the wall, and refused to be budged. From that night on he shared his dogsitter's bed.

Walks

Every dog loves its leash. It is the key to the outside world and a symbol of freedom, even though the dog gets tied to it. A leash means walks, adventure, encounters with other dogs, tracks and scents of other creatures, a chance to act out natural behavior, namely, running. This is all expressed in human terms, but it is meant to convey canine feelings about walks—if the walks are what they should be. For you can't keep a dog locked up in an apartment like a canary, a hamster, or a cat. You can't do it if for no other reason than the dog's digestive system. A dog has to relieve itself every few hours, and because it eats proteins, its urine and feces have a strong, unpleasant smell. Depending on the dog's size and breed, the amount of body waste may also be massive. Two pounds (1 kg) of meat results in at least 10.5 ounces (300 g) of feces.

Rules for Short Walks

You have to take your dog out at least four times a day for it to relieve itself properly and be comfortable staying in 10 to 12 hours at night. If you take it out less often, in a few years you'll have a dog with kidney problems.

Urinating: Every male dog—and sometimes females ranking high in the pack hierarchy—pass their urine in small portions spread out over a long route at spots where other dogs have relieved themselves. Ethologists (students of animal behavior) call this "marking," and being able to mark is important for a dog's self-esteem. This is a major reason that dogs have to be taken for walks (see page 66).

Walks— Where to?

In the country there is no problem. You take a short drive to a back road or to the woods and let the dog run on a long leash. You have to know your dog very well and be familiar with local conditions before considering letting your dog run free:

- Are there hunters around who'll shoot at anything that moves or are there farmers with ready guns?
- Is your dog the kind that may take off after deer or other game?
- Is the area in a rabies district? Here all dogs have to be kept on leashes, and you should carry your dog's vaccination certificate with you.

In the city things are more difficult. True, there are more smells to sniff here (greater dog population density), but there is also more car exhaust and traffic noise, and the dog cannot be let off the leash. The latter I don't find so tragic. In the city, we drive or walk to parks or to other green spaces frequented by dogs and their owners. Places like this offer a great opportunity for your dog to get acquainted with other dogs and learn canine etiquette (see page 58).

Your own backyard, no matter how large, is no substitute for the walk. Even if you let your dog run freely in the yard, this doesn't supply it with new sensory material, which every dog needs as mental stimulation. A yard is wonderful for letting the dog out first thing in the morning and last thing at night. The dog can also play there, but it can't leave scent marks, which is extremely important for a male dog's sense of self. Also, most dogs are reluctant to defecate in their own territory.

The balcony—but only in emergencies: There are people who let their dogs urinate on paper on the balcony. This is feasible only with a small dog and is acceptable only if the owner is too sick to go outside. Turning it into a permanent arrangement is wrong: Dogs that habitually relieve themselves on balconies are emotionally deprived.

Walks—How?

Going to the nearest street corner and back or once around the block does not count as a walk. A dog is by nature a runner and needs exercise. Four walks half an hour each is the minimum. A full hour's walk every weekday and longer hikes on the weekend would be nice. Of course, what kind of walk you take and how long it is depends on the dog's breed. Some dogs are less eager for exercise, and others get a proper workout only if they can run along next to a bicycle.

A Plea for Using a Leash

If you take your dog walking where there are lots of people, you should keep it on a leash out of consideration for others. (In some localities it may also be a legal requirement!) Most people don't appreciate a strange dog running up to them and sniffing them, let alone being jumped on. It matters very little whether the dog is large or small. People who are afraid of dogs don't care what the breed. And any breed perceived to be dangerous, like German shepherd dogs, Dobermans, or Great Danes, triggers a fear reaction that often expresses itself in inappropriate behavior—which is then misinterpreted by the dog. Many a dog has ended up biting in such a situation. Your protestations that Arko is really very gentle and has never hurt anyone will not cut much ice with the victim.

A Well-trained Walking Dog

It should not be too much to expect that one's dog always be under control and the owner considerate of other people. Only then can bias against dogs be countered. There are trials administered by dog sport clubs that are open to all breeds from dachshund to Irish wolfhound, and dogs that pass them get a certificate of "proper conduct in traffic."

A proper dog walk is a walk with and for the dog. That means that you won't cover as much distance as you might on your own. Instead you have to let the dog stop and sniff as much and as long as it feels like (see also page 68). You also have to let it meet other dogs. In such encounters with unfamiliar dogs the leash is more a hindrance than a help because the leash gives the dog an exaggerated sense of importance.

Retain authority: Although you want to give the dog some freedom, you should not give in to its every whim and let yourself be dragged from tree to tree. The prescription "It's smarter to give in than to insist on having one's way" doesn't work with dogs. Even though you are taking the walk for the dog's sake, you should still stay in charge. That is where the leash helps. It is a kind of extension of your arm, and a corrective yank—without any acccompanying words—should be firm, not tentative. This is the only way the dog will notice it. If the dog has responded properly, you can let the leash go slack again immediately after the yank.

If a dog rolls in mud, this may, depending on how potent the smell is, be the end of that walk. Take the dog home and give it a bath. Don't punish it except for an emphatic "Phooey!" for even the most civilized poodle is not impervious to the seductive aroma of rotting carrion, moldy lemon peel, or human feces. Dogs love smells we find offensive, and they like to wear them the way we like to try out perfume samples at the store. So let the dog's nose have its secret enjoyments. Explanations that dogs like to wear strange smells as camouflage or to cover foreign smells with their own are nothing more than speculation.

Physical Care of the Dog

Dogs should be groomed regularly and thoroughly not just for the sake of beauty but primarily for hygiene and comfort. Brushing the dog's coat, cleaning its ears, checking its teeth, and trimming its nails are all chores you take upon yourself when you get a dog.

Baths—When and How?

The warning not to bathe a dog until it is a year old and not to give it more baths than absolutely necessary belongs to the past. Now that there are nonalkaline dog shampoos, you can bathe your dog without worry, but you should observe the following rules:

Puppies should not be bathed until they are at least 12 weeks old and have had their first immunizations.

Grown dogs may be bathed every three months or whenever they reek. Bitches should get a bath after their heat period.

Frequent baths are not beneficial. Even mild shampoos wash some fat out of the fur, and it is the fat that accounts for the coat's excellent protective quality against cold, rain, and other effects of the elements.

The correct temperature of the bath water is 93°F (34°C). Be careful to keep water out of the dog's ears and suds out of its eyes. Very few dogs get into the tub or shower willingly, even if they are the kind that jumps into every stream or pond.

Dogs with long hair or a thick undercoat such as the chow chow, develop a strong "doggy" smell after being bathed. It is better to keep these dogs clean through daily brushing and combing without excessive massaging of the skin, and consequently the fat glands. Wash frequently those parts of the fur that get soaked with urine.

Thorough drying of the dog after a

A girl taking a Pyrenean mountain dog on a winter walk.

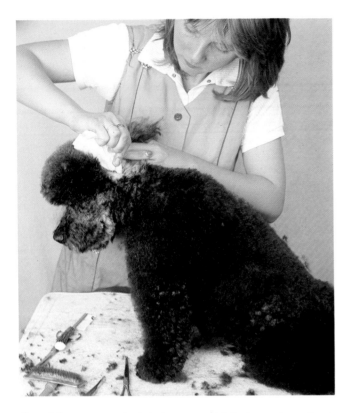

combed first because brushing alone does not keep their coat in shape. If you comb and brush the coat regularly, the fur can't get matted. Combing out matted fur hurts because it pulls the skin. Sometimes you have to resort to scissors, but try not to let things get that far. After brushing, you should rub the dog down with a slightly damp chamois cloth. This removes any leftover dust and gives the coat a nice shine.

3. When the dog is shedding, you should comb through the fur first with your bare hands, moving them against the lay of the hairs. You will probably end up with sore muscles in your hands from this, but it's the only way to get the dead hairs of the undercoat to the surface, where they can be brushed out easily. The head and paws have to be worked over the same way. Dead hairs make a dog itch terribly.

Even short-haired dogs shed and need to be groomed daily.

The Care of Eyes and Ears

The eyes should be wiped gently with a tissue if there is dried secretion in the corners. In breeds with drooping lower lids, such as basset hounds, bulldogs, and Saint Bernards, this is the case every day. Make sure that the secretion doesn't build up, for then it is harder to remove, and bare spots or inflammation may develop.

If the eyes get inflamed or very bloodshot or if the dog is blinking constantly or seems bothered by light, a visit to the veterinarian is in order.

The ears, especially if they are the long, droopy kind, are first cleaned with a damp cloth to remove dirt and bits of food. In long-haired breeds the ears are then combed. The inside of the ears should be checked regularly, every two weeks for dogs with lop or folded ears, especially if the ears are very hairy. Pull up the ear and clean the entrance to auditory canal carefully with a cotton swab dipped in oil. If there is any sign of redness, you should call the veterinarian. You may want to let your veterinarian perform the first ear check so that you can watch how it's done.

One of the most important grooming chores—especially for dogs with lop ears—is cleaning the ears. In some breeds the ears have to be checked every day. In this picture, a poodle is getting its ears cleaned.

bath is important. Rub the entire animal down carefully; dogs enjoy this. Avoid drafts, and let the dog run until it is thoroughly dry.

Care of the Coat

I don't want to give specific instructions here on how to use shearing machines, trimming knives, thinning shears, currycombs, and the like. If your dog is of a breed that requires the use of these tools, your breeder will tell you so, and you will have to learn how to perform the chores properly. Here are a few basic rules:

1. No dog objects to daily brushing if it's done with sensitivity and with a firm brush whose bristles don't scratch. You should spend 15 to 30 minutes a day on this task, depending on the kind of coat. The brushing not only removes dead hair from the coat but also provides a time of closeness between you and your pet. To the dog, brushing feels very much like vigorous petting.

2. Long-haired dogs have to be

Regular Checking of the Teeth

The teeth of dogs are stronger than those of humans. Dogs practically never get cavities, but buildup of tartar is all the more common, especially in small dogs and when the owner neglects to look after the dog's teeth.

Dental care for dogs means:

- Getting a young puppy used to having its teeth scrubbed with water and a cloth.
- Cleaning the dog's teeth with a soft brush and a toothpaste the dog likes or unscented soap (when the dog is grown). There are special dental care products for dogs.
- Visiting the veterinarian regularly so that the removal of tartar is painless. A heavy buildup of tartar can cause pain and inflammations. If a dog has bad breath, the presence of decay-promoting bacteria has already reached such proportions that tooth extraction is often necessary.

The Care of Claws and Pads

Claws have to be cut if a dog does not wear them down sufficiently by walking on roads. The dewclaws especially need trimming because they don't get any wear from walking. If a dewclaw grows into a hook, it can get caught in the collar. If this happens the dog may panic and hurt itself (see Glossary, DEWCLAWS). Claws are "alive," meaning that they contain blood vessels and nerves. Only the tip is dead. In light-colored claws it is possible to distinguish the live from the dead part, but not in dark claws. It is important when trimming claws not to cut into the live tissue. I let the veterinarian trim my dogs' claws because I don't feel quite brave enough to try it myself.

The care of the pads is especially important. A dog runs around on them all day, so they get a lot of use. In wet weather or snow, the pads should be wiped with a damp cloth and dried off every day. Check frequently that there is no chewing gum

A Yorkshire terrier during its bath routine: rinsing after soaping, then being carefully rubbed dry.

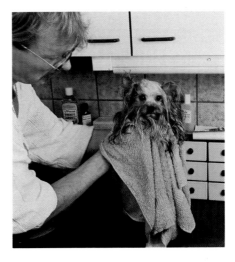

stuck to the pads or small pebbles, splinters, or other objects lodged between them. If the pads are sore from running, they should be powdered; if they are cracked, put petroleum jelly on them (see also page 42).

The Rear End—A Dog's Visiting Card

Cleaning the rear end is part of grooming, because sometimes dogs dirty themselves. This is best done with a damp cloth. Be sure to remove all traces of feces from the fur of long-haired dogs.

If a dog *drags its rear end along the ground*, this has nothing to do with a dirty behind or with marking. It is a sign that the

A Welsh terrier is getting trimmed (above) and having its nails clipped (below).

anal glands are full and clogged. This is not only an unpleasant sensation for the dog but also a severe social handicap in encounters with other dogs. For the anal glands secrete substances with potent odors that reveal everything about a dog's identity to other canines. That is why dogs like to sniff the underneath of each other's tails (see page 59). Clogged anal glands should be drained by the veterinarian.

Pests

When a dog keeps scratching itself, you should check it for parasites. The dog may have fleas, ticks (see Glossary, DOG FLEAS AND TICKS), or lice that are almost too small to see. Lice glue their eggs to the hairs of the fur. Have the vet diagnose the pests and prescribe appropriate medication.

Important: Playing with the Dog

Play is a great aid in teaching a puppy, and it is a crucial form of social contact between the dog and its master. Playing is a kind of therapy in which the aggressive tendencies inherent in dogs can find release.

Playing with humans is especially important for dogs that spend a lot of time alone. In the course of play dogs also learn new ways to occupy themselves and how to play without their humans now and then.

Play as an Aid in Training

Puppies require as much love as babies do, if they are to grow up into happy and normal dogs. In other words, you have to spend a lot of time with your puppy, and spending time means playing.

Some Brief Observations on the Nature of Play

- Play has no conscious purpose beyond itself. An object is dragged around for no particular reason; a dog tries to catch its own tail, and so on.
- Curiosity, the desire to explore new

things and new situations, is an important element of play. This shows that play is an active form of learning. Make use of this fact in the training of your dog.

- Puppies have a short attention span when they play. Anything new is more interesting than whatever they happen to be doing. What this means for you is that one toy or one kind of game is not enough. Take advantage of the large selection of toys at pet stores but check that the toy is made of suitable material (see page 22).
- As a dog gets older, it gets more absorbed in whatever it is doing. Make use of this trait in the course of training.

Note: Puppies play most actively with their litter mates. If there are no litter mates, you have to serve as substitute. But humans are poor substitutes because they are humans rather than dogs. Dogs have to be able to play with other dogs to learn to express themselves as canines. That is why you should take even a little puppy to a park or field where other dogs play, even if you live in the city.

Play as Social Contact

Dogs and humans are among the few creatures that still play even as adults. Let me pass along an observation here from the field of ethology: Just as dogs are wolves that never quite grew up, humans are apes that failed to grow up (see Glossary, NEOTENY). Almost all breeds of dogs enjoy playing even in old age (boxers, Airedale terriers, and spaniels, for example). Play is initiated with a posture that resembles a bow: The head and front of the body rest on the front legs with the chest touching the ground, and the tail end sticks up high on straight legs. At the same time the dog moves forward in jerks as though trying to say, "Come on...let's go!" The face wears its "play expression" with the mouth slightly open and the lips stretched as though for laughing.

The next gesture of invitation is "pretend carrying." The dog picks up a stick or a ball and deposits it in front of the partner. If you reach down for the object, the dog quickly grabs it and and runs off with it.

Forms of play with a partner:

1. Approaching and running away (see "pretend carrying").
2. Running in circles (a sign of intense desire for play).
3. Playing tag.
4. All forms of wrestling and playful fighting.
5. Fetching and bringing objects.

It is particularly important to engage in the wrestling and playful fighting forms of play with a puppy so that it learns to control "play biting." Puppies have no inhibiting mechanism for biting, and since biting is part of playful fighting, they have to be taught to restrain themselves. I use the following items for games that involve wrestling and running:

- a solid rag for tugging and shaking;
- a thick glove for wrestling and letting the dog bite;
- a soccer or volley ball (more useful than a tennis ball) for intercepting, stopping, or rolling in front of one's feet;
- a stick for biting, jumping over, running after, fetching, and bringing back.

Other shared games:

- You run off and the dog runs after you, trying, as it did with its mother, to bite your heels and stop you (see Glossary, HEAL NIPPING).
- You can play Frisbee with your dog. A dog that has learned how to do it tries to catch the Frisbee in midair. The Frisbee should have a soft edge. You can also buy special Frisbees for dogs.
- You can run a crosscountry obstacle course with your dog or simply jog together.

Play as Therapy

Dogs need opportunities to vent the aggressive energies within them. This is especially true of terriers that are kept exclusively as pets. Terriers that don't have enough to occupy them start looking for substitute quarry and will chase anything, from the moving wheels of a bicycle or small motorcycle to the legs of a passerby, playing children, or a hapless cat.

Therapy: To keep aggressive energies from building up too much, you should play with your dog a lot. The best game is to have a tug of war over some prize such as a burlap bag, an old towel, or a stick. *Never* wrestle with your dog over the leash! If your dog comes to think of the leash as an object of quarry, you will no longer be able to walk it properly. Dogs love these tussles; they yank and pull and growl and bark and run away with the quarry, thus working off their natural aggressiveness in small, harmless bits. But make sure that you stay in charge of the game so that the all-important order of dominance between master and dog remains intact.

Living Arrangements with a Dog

There are three possible living arrangements:

1. In a rented apartment (under this option I include a furnished room if a person is permitted to keep a dog there) or a condominium apartment.

2. A house without a yard, which from the dog's point of view is the same as an apartment.

3. A house with a garden or backyard, which represents the ideal situation for a dog.

A Dog in an Apartment or a House without a Yard

Of course there are the most varied possibilities under this category, ranging from a single room to a spacious penthouse and from a first-floor apartment to one high up in a high-rise building, and they all differ in the quality of life they offer a dog. But here are a few basic rules for choosing an apartment dog:

- The larger the city, the smaller the dog.
- The larger the apartment building, the smaller the dog.
- The more stairs there are to climb, the more "normal" the dog's legs should be. (Dachshunds and English bulldogs are examples of breeds that develop leg problems.)
- The less leisure time you have, the less

Opposite page: A playing dog is a happy dog. An Airedale terrier in an expectant play posture.

grooming to keep the dog's coat clean and healthy should be required.
- The less opportunity for long walks, the more sedate the breed.
- The more persons live in the building, the less the breed should be given to barking.

The Problems of Having an Apartment Dog

By an apartment dog I mean a dog that spends much time alone and whose people go out to work. Such solitary dogs tend to develop behavior problems. There is no breed adapted to living in solitude. All dogs are sociable by nature. If you decide you simply cannot do without a dog in spite of all this, consider the following:

- Your decision to get a dog has to be well-considered, not a momentary whim.
- You have to be prepared to spend all your free time with the dog. Hardly being home during the week and then going off without the dog on the weekend is inexcusable.
- You should have a normal work day so that your dog never has to be alone for more than eight hours.
- The dog has to have a permanent exclusive place in the apartment where it feels at home.
- The dog has to be well trained and have a strong sense of self to endure this unnatural state of solitude. You have to build up its self-confidence with much praise, success experiences, and physical affection.
- Try making a doghouse for your dog in the apartment. It is an ideal refuge for the dog, familiar, exclusive, and permanent. I've known some dogs with behavioral problems that overcame their bad habits and calmed down once they had a dog house.

Response to Behavior Problems

Dogs that destroy things, bark incessantly, or lapse from being housebroken when left alone should not be scolded or punished when you come home. The dog

is delighted to see you again and associates any form of punishment only with the here and now, not with what it might have done an hour ago. Try instead to protect furniture you are worried about and give the dog a bone for chewing when it is bored. If new bad habits arise all of a sudden, try to figure out what might have caused them (see also Abnormal Behavior in Dogs, page 101).

Are two dogs an alternative? Since I'm opposed to one dog being confined in an apartment, I can't really recommend getting two dogs that are then left alone. However, if two dogs get along well and complement each other, things may work out quite well.

Max the Letter Shredder

*Max is a poodle living with his mistress in a city apartment. He is a playful, not particularly flashy, but affectionate and obedient dog. When his mistress took a part-time job working half days, everything went well for two weeks. But then Max started to shred the letters and newspa-*pers that the mailman stuck through the mail slot. Max felt slighted by the incomprehensible change in his daily life, and he protested by tearing up the mail. Besides, he had always been allowed to play with the newspaper once his mistress was through with it. This story has a happy ending: The woman was allowed to take her dog to work with her.*

A Dog in a House with a Backyard

Such a dog is lucky. It can get out when it wants to, though you should not get into the habit of playing doorkeeper for your dog and letting it in or out every time it barks. You read earlier that using a yard is no substitute for dog walks, but a yard is useful for a quick run outside when the dog has to relieve itself. If people have to pass through the yard to get to your door, lock the gate to the yard or put up a sign warning that there is a dog on the premises, no matter how small the dog. Some people are afraid of all dogs. The sign should not read "Caution: Biting Dog" (a dog that bites is not something to brag about) but rather something like "Collie Guarding This House."

A fence has to be provided that your dog cannot jump over or crawl under. Dogs running loose are not popular and often don't live long.

The mailbox should be located by the gate to the yard, because dogs and mail carriers have a notoriously poor relationship. (See Glossary, MAIL CARRIERS).

A Dog That Lives Outside

Anybody who plans to keep a dog outdoors all the time has to be sure to choose the right breed.

Important: The following rules apply if a dog is kept outdoors:

1. The thicker the fur and the undercoat, the easier it is to keep a dog outside. (Friends of mine have a chow chow that enjoys its outdoor doghouse in the snow.)

2. An outdoor dog has to get accustomed to being outdoors when young and be hardened gradually. Indoor dogs, especially short-haired ones, are no longer

Even more pleasurable than sleeping in one's own basket is curling up on a sofa or armchair. Shown in this picture is a basset hound blissfully asleep.

suitable for living outside.

3. No family dog should be kept exclusively outdoors. Such a dog needs contact with the family and occasional periods indoors.

The dog house should be the right size for the dog. It has to be absolutely draft-free and have enough bedding for the dog to make a nest for itself. Straw is best for warmth but not hygienic. You can buy appropriate doghouses and cages through pet supply firms.

An outdoor run is very practical if you have a yard. An indoor dog can be kept there a few hours a day without supervision except during inclement weather or when it's exceptionally cold. The run should be partially shaded, have a place where the dog can dig a hole for itself (for resting as in nature), and contain clean sand. Before you build a run it would be best to get information on the subject from the dog club of your dog's breed.

Note: Leaving your dog outside on a leash for a while so that it can watch the world without running off is not the same as keeping it chained all the time.

Dogs and Children

Although many dogs are naturally fond of children and are very gentle with little ones, not every dog is suited for living with children. Here, too, it is more a question of individual personality than breed. Let me give two examples:

Example #1: German shepherd dogs have a strong urge to protect their people and are eager to learn and subordinate themselves to a master. These are good qualities for a dog with children, but there are some German shepherds with a strong-willed character that need equally strong-willed masters. If you have such a dog and move it into a small city apartment, it can become dangerous to children.

Example #2: Chow chows can sometimes be self-willed to the point of obstructiveness, and they are quiet loners. These breed characteristics don't sound very promising for a dog living with children. Yet, when a chow and a child grow up together, a deep and lasting friendship can develop between the two that is rarely found with other breeds. For chows form a primary bond with one person, to whom they remain forever faithful.

The living arrangements are crucial when you choose a dog to live with children. The right dog for a house with a yard can be the wrong dog in an apartment building. The right dog for sharing a household with active, outgoing children may be all wrong for a quiet, sensitive child. It's best if a child and a dog can grow up together, for then there develops a closeness similar to that between siblings of one litter.

Qualities in a Dog Living with Children

- It should not be nervous or excessively timid.

Children from about eight years on can be assigned responsibility for some of the grooming chores. Corinne is brushing her Yorkshire terrier mongrel.

- It must be very good-natured.
- It should not be sensitive to noise.
- It should be playful and not easily tire of playing.
- It should not mind being pushed around a bit and should not respond immediately with defensive behavior (specialists call this having a high threshold of tolerance; see Glossary, THRESHOLD OF TOLERANCE.) At the same time it should not put up with oppressive tyranny.
- It should have a natural protector instinct.

Most of these qualities are found in dogs belonging to large breeds. Large dogs tend to be good-natured, hardly ever bite out of fear, are quiet by nature and rarely nervous, and are good protectors that know their own strength.

This does not mean that you should let your child run up to every large strange dog. There are quite a few Saint Bernards that don't like children. And if your child is not used to dogs, it may suddenly get frightened and through its behavior trigger a fear or attack response in the dog.

Large dogs have the disadvantage that they need a lot of room and a yard. They are not meant for city life, and they are so strong that a child cannot hold them back in certain situations.

Dogs for Children

Large dogs for children: Golden retrievers, Labrador retrievers, Old English sheepdogs, collies, Bernese mountain dogs, Hungarian herding dogs (kuvasz and komondor), Belgian sheep dogs, rottweilers, Hovawarts, Airedale terriers, boxers, and German shepherd dogs. (However, there are German shepherds that don't want anything to do with children.) Further, boxers and German shepherds can be recommended only with reservations, because they tend to fight with other dogs and have to be very well trained for a child to be able to manage one alone on a walk.)

Very large breeds like Saint Bernards and Newfoundlands, also get along with children, but they require even more space than the breeds listed above.

Medium-sized dogs for children: Cocker spaniels, standard schnauzers, and beagles. Fox terriers, Irish terriers, and Bedlington terriers can be very temperamental, and they, too, tend to fight with other dogs.

Small dogs for children: Wirehaired dachshunds, Welsh corgis, cairn terriers, and French bulldogs are suitable for children that are not too rambunctious.

Of course crossbreeds fitting into the various categories can be kept with children, too.

A Dog as a Pedagogical Factor

Psychologists, educators, and pediatricians all agree that dogs have a pedagogic value in the development of children. A child and a dog—this is mutual pedagogy at work. Both learn from each other; they do it through play; and their emotional involvement in the process is great. A dog helps develop a child's sense of responsibility and conscientiousness, and it occasions lessons in learning to be considerate, orderly, and punctual. And that is not all:

A Dog as Teacher of Social Behavior

This may look like a bit of an exaggeration at first glance, but it is true that a child's relationship with a dog can offer character-forming experiences with duties, love, birth, and death.

This is what it looks like in practice: A child wishes for a dog, a creature with an astonishing ability to communicate and an inborn need to be a loyal follower. The child, of course, is not aware of this. It sees in the dog an object on which to lavish its affections, a living toy, somebody that is always there. Parents get a dog as playmate and protector for the child, as a source of amusement during times of boredom, and as a companion for an only child.

The parents play the crucial role in how the relationship between dog and child will work out, a relationship that will have an impact on the child into adulthood.

A friendship with a dog significantly lessens a child's communication difficulties with other children; this is a special boon to an only child. Walking with a dog on a leash gives one a sense of self-worth and leads to contact with other people without requiring any special effort. Children that have a dog to talk to seldom remain mute in the presence of other children (or of adults). A dog partly compensates for not having siblings and playmates. Besides, playmates are easier to find if one has a dog.

A Dog as Therapy for Handicapped Children

What is simply a wonderful opportunity for healthy, normal children can be necessary therapy for handicapped children. There are many positive reports of such experiences in the United States and England. Mentally disturbed persons learn through physical closeness to make revitalizing mental and emotional contact with the surrounding world.

With physically handicapped children a dog can foster self-confidence and relieve some of the mental stress. A dog is a playmate that is unaware of handicaps and pays no attention to them. A dog is always cheerful and generates happiness. Dogs also help break the ice with other children, which can be difficult otherwise.

How Little Pete Learned to Walk

Pete suffered from cerebral palsy and obstinately refused to walk because he often fell down and got hurt when he tried. Then his father bought a puppy for him, and he forgot fear and caution, following the dog from room to room, sometimes stumbling and falling, sometimes on all fours, and sometimes walking upright. This in itself was almost miraculous. In addition, Pete's sense of self-worth got a big boost; he no longer needed constant proof of love from his parents, because he was so proud of himself and busy taking

A dog is more than just a toy that's alive. It is a playmate and a creature to relate to.

A dog enjoys the outdoors even in winter. Here an Irish wolfhound is bounding through the snow.

care of his little dog. He also found it easier to talk to his siblings, for now he had something to talk about that everybody was interested in: "our dog."

A child and a dog form a twosome. That makes the child feel strong and independent, whether the child is healthy or sick.

Rules for Cold and Hot Days

Winter Time

Winter raises some special questions and requires some changes in grooming.

In what month should your dog's coat be clipped or trimmed? Do it in October and don't have the fur cut too short. Dogs also should not be bathed during the winter.

Should you let your dog out less when it is cold? Dry cold is not as unpleasant as wet and cold weather. Dogs that like to run are less sensitive to the cold than ones that move slowly, and long-haired dogs feel the cold less than short-haired ones.

A coat for winter? When it's damp and cold outside, putting a coat on an older, smooth-haired dog that is used to living in a warm apartment can help protect your pet against colds and rheumatism (see page 22).

Preventing colds? After a walk in cold and wet weather it's a good idea to rub the dog down with a towel and use a hair-dryer (if the dog likes it). Dogs can catch colds or urinary tract infections just the way we do.

Dogs and cross-country skiing? Take along on cross-country trails only long-legged dogs that have been trained properly for this (by running along next to a bicycle during the summer). And please take other cross-country skiers into consideration!

Care of pads: Rub some oil or cold cream onto the dog's pads before a walk in the snow and bathe the paws in warm water or camomile tea when you return. This also helps protect the pads against

road salt.

Eating snow: Dogs like to eat snow, but it is not good for them. Eating snow causes diarrhea, and if too much is eaten on an empty stomach, gastritis accompanied by cramps and vomiting can result. Gastritis requires treatment by the veterinarian.

Summer Time

When the weather gets hot, you have to observe the following:

Fresh water is something you should always provide, no matter what time of year. But in the summer you have to check the water bowl more often and replenish the water as needed.

Food: Don't worry if your dog is eating less than usual. We, too, have less appetite during hot weather.

A shady place: Be sure that your dog has a shady place in the yard. Most dogs like lying in the sun, but every so often they want to move to the shade where it's cooler.

Walks: Take long dog walks early in the morning or in the late afternoon or evening. Walking when the sun beats down isn't good for you or the dog.

The car: Be sure that you park the car in the shade and that there is a constant supply of fresh air. The temperature inside a car can quickly rise to unbearable and dangerous levels.

Bathing: Most dogs like to take a dip in a stream or lake. Dry them off enough afterwards so that they will not get other people wet when shaking.

A Dog in the City

People who would like to ban dogs from cities present two supporting arguments:

1. The poor dogs should not be expected to live in cities at all because they are not suited for such a life.

2. Dogs and what they leave behind are a serious threat to public health.

Both arguments are flawed and exaggerated. Let us consider each of them in turn.

The Poor City Dogs

According to a survey of veterinarians, the dogs that are presently living in cities are no sicker than dogs living in smaller towns or in the country. To be sure, cities with their noise, exhaust fumes, and limited opportunities for walks are far from a paradise for dogs. But they are no paradise for people either. Dogs have proven to be extremely adaptable creatures, and they have adjusted to city life, too. Their important advantage is that they are living with people who are true dog lovers. After all, who else would put up with the problems of owning a dog in the city?

The Matter of Dog Excreta

There are people who claim that dog excretions in the streets make life in the city miserable. Not the streets clogged with cars, not the clouds of car exhaust, not the mountains of paper and plastic trash—no, the dog feces and urine are the number one complaint. Sensational headlines occasionally stir up hysteria over dog excreta. Yet where are dogs supposed to relieve themselves? The curb next to the sidewalk is taken up by parked cars, and a solution like the one in Paris—which has no-parking zones in some areas where dogs can be walked—is unlikely in the USA. Yet the curb was not originally designed for parked cars but for dirt and trash. Public parks have become places for people to picnic and sunbathe. It is truly getting difficult to find a place where a dog can relieve itself discreetly. Plain old earth and grass are best because the feces disintegrate fastest there. By this I do not mean the sand in children's playgrounds! It is unforgivable to take one's dog to a playground in the early morning and late at night because it will relieve itself there so quickly and easily. The same is true of any public area where people congregate. Apart from the fact that this kind of behavior plays into the hands of dog opponents, it's hygienically irresponsible.

A Plea for Dogs in Cities

On the one hand there is the frustrated dog owner and on the other the dogless city dweller stepping onto dog feces more and more often. To the latter the former's rational and appeasing explanations carry little weight. Yet the two have to live side by side. A dog often is the sole companion a person has. It can also be a link to nature that city people badly need. Let's remember the children who would have no first-hand experience with the natural world if it were not for dogs, and let's think of those who want to live with a dog out of a love for dogs, a need for contact and affection, or a desire to get exercise every day and take long walks on weekends.

In many localities, "pooper-scooper" laws now provide the answer: The owner is *required* to clean up after his or her pet. But even where there isn't a statute on the books, many responsible pet owners have learned that the simplest solution is to carry a plastic bag that can be turned inside-out over the hand, used to grasp the deposit, pulled right-side out again, sealed, and discarded in a trash can.

My conclusion: If you really want to have a dog, you should not let yourself be talked out of it.

The Dog—An Independent Creature

In an Austrian brochure entitled *All About Dogs*, I found the following "Ten Things a Dog Asks of Its People."

1. My life is likely to last 10 to 15 years. Any separation from you will be painful for me. Remember that before you buy me.

2. Give me time to understand what you want of me.

3. Place your trust in me—it's crucial for my well-being.

4. Don't be angry at me for long, and don't lock me up as a punishment. You have your work, your entertainment, and your friends. I have only you.

5. Talk to me sometimes. Even if I don't understand your words I understand your voice when it's speaking to me.

6. Be aware that however you treat me, I'll never forget it.

7. Remember before you hit me that I have teeth that could easily crush the bones of your hand but that I choose not to bite you.

8. Before you scold me for being "uncooperative," "obstinate," or "lazy," ask yourself if something might be bothering me. Perhaps I'm not getting the right food, or I've been out in the sun too long, or my heart is getting old and weak.

9. Take care of me when I get old; you, too, will grow old.

10. Go with me on difficult journeys. Never say: "I can't bear to watch it" or "Let it happen in my absence." Everything is easier for me if you are there.

I subscribe fully and whole-heartedly to all this. Only number 5 seems to me understated. Talk to your dog a lot, as much as you can, always. The sound of your voice creates harmony between you and your dog, and talking is good for you, too, especially if you live alone.

Remarks on the Subject "Wolf"

Erik Zimen, a biologist whose specialty is the study of wolves and dogs, spent three years observing a wolf pack and a lot of standard poodles. He analyzed and counted the animals' activities and behavior patterns. The wolves engaged in 362 different activities, of which the poodles retained about two thirds. The poodles had lost only the ones that were no longer of use in living with people. As this indicates, you will be able to understand your dog better if you know some basic facts about wolves.

- In a wolf pack there is a well-defined social hierarchy that ranges from the position of pack leader, which can be occupied by a female, to that of an underling who serves as scapegoat. The young are raised by the whole pack, and some kind of biologically controlled birth control is in effect.

- There is what we would call babysitting. Wolves of lower rank look after the pups when a higher-ranking mother wolf goes off on a hunt.

- Several generations of a family live together in a system that is primarily

oriented to protect the pack as a whole.

- Any creatures that live together in such an organized fashion have to have clear means of communication. Since wild animals have to be quiet, their many signals are visual: posture, movement of different body parts—especially the tail and ears—and clearly defined facial expressions. By these means the animals are able to convey the most subtle moods and impulses. All the forms of expression are part of minutely defined rituals and add up to a strictly observed set of social rules that often determine social rank. As Zimen puts it: "You can tell what a wolf means by looking at it."
- When wolves howl—they hardly ever bark—this is neither a warning nor a complaint. Howling helps guide lost members back to the pack and enhances the sense of belonging together. It expresses a friendly mood and the pleasure of companionship. You could say that it's comparable to people singing together.
- The team spirit of a pack becomes evident when the wolves catch the scent of prey. The animals crowd together, and all the noses point in the direction of the prey, as if the entire pack were one "supernose." A few seconds of rigid immobility, and then they're off; the chase is on.

So much about wolves.

What You Can Learn from This for Living with Your Dog

- The most important thing is probably the pack feeling, which some breeds, such as poodles, have transferred in its entirety to humans. A dog needs its people; it is happy only in their presence. Keep that in mind if you have to leave your dog alone a lot.
- Learn to understand what your dog is trying to tell you. It is speaking with its ears, its fur, and its tail (see pages 65 and 66).
- Not just males but females, too, can be alpha animals (see Glossary, ALPHA ANIMALS) and can try to become boss of a

human family.

- Make sure that the hierarchy within your family remains intact and the dog does not take over the role of boss.
- A mother dog expects you to assist her in raising her young. Dogs believe in team spirit and expect the same of us.
- When dogs are trying to warn us or tell us something, they bark. They have learned that in the course of living with us, and barking has become part of their language (see page 62).
- When dogs howl

they are calling for their pack, if they are left alone too much;

they are calling for a sexual partner, if there is a female in heat anywhere in the neighborhood;

they are singing their age-old chorus; it's their form of making music.

The Partnership between Dog and Human

A dog is not a mechanical toy nor a stuffed animal to pet and squeeze. It is an independent creature and—in spite of the fact that it has subjugated itself to humans the way no other animal has—it is still subject to the ancient laws of predators. The partnership between human and dog is based on mutual consent, so true friendship is possible with a dog. A bond is formed that goes way beyond mere living together and having become used to each other. A mutual understanding develops that often requires no spoken words or outward signs.

The prerequisite for such a close relationship between man and dog is that you regard your dog not as a four-legged burglar alarm, or a toy for the children, or a status symbol, but as a true partner—without losing sight of the fact that a dog is still a dog and therefore different from humans. While developing

Opposite page: A high leap straight up from standing position. Two mixed-breed dachshunds during their daily play and training session.

Two dog owners meeting on a walk should hold their dogs' leashes as shown in the picture.

such a close bond to humans, dogs have retained their essential dog nature.

According to ethologist Erik Zimen: "The attachment dogs form to their humans is matched by the attachment of people to their dogs. If we disregard the occasional shocking cases where human minds gone awry create physically and psychologically abnormal dogs, we may assert that the partnership between person and dog is mutual. Dogs help people, and people allow dogs to remain dogs by letting them express their instinct for play, movement, and reproduction. What keeps fascinating me about dogs is this: the animal's tremendous dependency on humans and its simultaneous independence; its joy in being alive and its uncanny ability to see right through its master or mistress."

And yet dogs have remained dogs; they are still "social predators," just as their ancestors the wolves were. That is their astonishing and delightful quality. Shortly after birth, dogs, "the wild beasts," are integrated into a social union of hu-

mans—a species that is totally alien to them—and form a very close bond with them. Their human comrade feeds them, takes care of their young, protects them against wind and weather, treats their diseases, and—with some exceptions, to be sure—chooses their sexual partners for them. In spite of all this, dogs have retained their own independent nature. This is something that never ceases to amaze me, just as the dog's sensory capacities, which are so different from ours, do. Let us now take a look at how a dog perceives the world.

Why Dogs Make Good Watchdogs

You are sitting at home reading the paper. Everything is peaceful and quiet. Suddenly your dog, which has been fast asleep, raises its head and starts growling. When the doorbell rings, the dog barks. Long before the bell rang it heard that a stranger was approaching. Because dogs' hearing is so acute, people have assigned them the role of watchdog.

A Dog's Ears

A dog hears much more than we do. It can detect sounds that are beyond our range of hearing. The human ear perceives sound waves in frequencies from about 16,000 to 20,000 vibrations per second, whereas dogs can hear up to between 70,000 and 100,000. Soundless dog whistles, which emit frequencies in the ultrasonic range, take advantage of this facet of a dog's hearing. Dogs have 17 muscles to move their ears, and dogs with natural prick ears (see Glossary, PRICK EARS) are able to turn their ears like radar receptors toward the source of sounds.

A Dog's Nose

When a dog investigates a human being or a member of its own species, its nose is always foremost. The nose tells it whether a person is familiar, whether it's someone sympathetic, or whether it's someone to guard against. The same is true in approaching other dogs. There are dogs that can't stand each other from the moment they catch the first scent (see page 00).

Its amazing sense of smell enables a dog to
- follow the track of game and bring it to bay (as a hunting dog);
- pick up the scent of a criminal, find a lost child, or detect narcotics in the most unlikely hiding places (as a police dog);
- find people buried under as much as 23 feet (7 m) of snow or rubble (as a rescue dog searching for victims after avalanche or earthquake catastrophes; see also Glossary, OLFACTORY AREA.

A dog sees the world through its nose: Our most important sensory organs, through which we take in our surroundings and which tell us what the world looks like, are our eyes. In a dog the nose

fulfills this function. We can't begin to imagine what kinds of things a dog's nose can sense. Here are a few "inconceivable" examples:
- A dog can smell whether or not we like it and if we are angry, sad, or afraid
- It can smell our inner agitation when we are evasive.
- When it follows our track, it knows how old the track is and the direction in which it goes.
- By sniffing on street corners, lampposts, trees, and car tires it learns what dogs passed there earlier and it leaves messages of its own. That's why we should allow our dogs time to sniff on walks (see also page 68).
- Of course your dog knows your specific smell very well. But you should not confuse it by continually changing your perfume or after-shave lotion.

Other evidence of the keenness of a dog's nose is how the animal sniffs the air. The nose is raised high into the wind to pick up scent particles that float in the air.

When you get a new dog, whether a

A watchdog (Airedale terrier). The sign on the gate says in Latin: Beware of the dog.

CAVE CANEM

puppy or a grown dog, you should stay with the same toiletries for the first six months and not change your scent personality. Only this way can your dog really get to know your smell. And one more request: Please don't wear strong perfume. If you do, this is a constant irritation to the dog's nose. Always keep in mind that though the dog is living in the same environment as you, it has its own, completely different sensory world.

The Sense of Taste

A dog's sense of taste has not been studied extensively, but it is intimately connected to the sense of smell. The preference for certain kinds of food is undoubtedly influenced by the sense of smell. The tongue (where the taste buds are located) has two additional functions in dogs:

- Because it is so mobile, the tongue can be used for drinking.
- A dog's tongue fulfills the same function as sweating does for us: It helps lower body temperature. When a dog pants, water evaporates from the tongue. Thus the tongue takes the place of sweat glands, which dogs lack almost entirely.

Why Dogs Respond to Movement

If you are downwind of a dog when it approaches you, that is, if it cannot smell you, it has to rely on its eyes. Dogs are by nature farsighted and therefore primarily equipped optically to perceive movement—a holdover from their past as hunting wolves. (This should serve as a warning to you and your child never to run away from a dog. It's the running that awakens the hunting instinct in a dog.) If you stand without moving, your dog will not see you until it is almost on top of you. Then it will respond quickly and almost automatically. It is the ability to see movement that hunt-

ers make use of in retrievers and pointers, and it is this same ability that enables Seeing Eye dogs to guide blind persons safely across busy streets and through crowds. Greyhounds can detect the the most minute movement a long distance away, and because of their narrow heads they have an angle of vision of about 270 degrees, which allows them to see even backward.

A Dog's Eyes

The field of vision of dogs (see Glossary, FIELD OF VISION) is larger than that of humans, but their three-dimensional vision is fairly limited. Dogs see better in dim light because of a reflective layer at the back of the eyes, which makes a dog's eyes light up when light strikes them. This structure of the eye allows a dog to perceive movement even in the dark. What it is that moves is revealed by the sense of smell, since dogs take in the world through their noses. I'm reminded of this every day now that my dog has gone blind. He is not nearly as handicapped as a blind person. When we go on walks together—I always keep him on a leash to be able to warn him of upcoming obstacles—nobody could tell that he is blind. He walks along briskly, following his nose, and sniffs around as he always did. The only difference is that he doesn't catch sight of other dogs at a distance, but only smells them when they are relatively close.

The Sense of Touch

A dog's whiskers, which are lodged deep in the skin, have some tactile function because they are connected to nerve cells. But they are far less important for a dog than whiskers are for cats. Other zones that have cells sensitive to touch are the lips, the paws, and the front of the nose (see Glossary, NOSE LEATHER).

The Swedish scientist, Dr. Zottermann, has discovered that there is a kind of receptor for infrared radiation in a dog's nose. This could explain why dogs are able to detect people who are buried alive in snow but they cannot detect buried frozen bodies.

What a Dog Can Tell by Its Senses

Through the combined use of their senses dogs are capable of some achievements that are quite astonishing to us creatures of civilization with our dulled senses.

- A dog can tell ahead of time that we are planning to leave.
- A dog that is fast asleep in spite of a blaring television will wake up instantly if, for instance, we rise from the chair in which we are sitting or rustle a food wrapper.
- Sled dogs are able to keep true to the direction they are traveling in at night, something skiers can't manage even with a compass.
- Dogs love looking down from a window onto a street (in the city) or watching the world from a raised post (in the country), even though some scientists tell us that their vision is not very good.
- A dog can distinguish the sound of its family's car from that of other cars.
- A dog can determine that you are approaching even before you have become visible.

These are abilities and accomplishments we can only partially explain. They demonstrate that we are living with a creature endowed by nature with senses that might enable it to survive in the wild even after centuries of domesticaiton.

Trotting along next to a bicycle is one of the best ways for a dog to get the exercise it needs. Shown is a blond male Hovawart.

Double spread on following pages: A pointer in typical pose with the nose held high into the wind.

Dogs and Their Behavior

When we live with a dog, we notice reactions that seem very "human" to us. We tend to remark on this when a dog reacts in a way we didn't expect of an animal. But what is "typically human" or "typically doglike"? The psychological reactions of man and dog to a situation can be very similar. When I was studying biology, a new science was emerging that dealt with the psyche of animals, and this new field of study was appropriately named "animal psychology."

Today this area of biology is thriving. Renamed ethology, or the study of animal behavior, it is often reported on in the popular press.

What Is Ethology?

Ethology is the study not only of animal behavior, but also of human behavior (behavior is the way a creature acts and reacts to things). Ethology takes special account of evolutionary development. The student of ethology asks: How did certain movements, utterances, and postures originate? What gave rise to them, and what do they mean?

Applied to dogs this means: What are dogs trying to tell us through their typical behavior—when they wag their tails, raise their hackles, prick their ears, jump up, or bark? How can we learn to understand our dog's real nature, its means of expression, its needs? I shall try to convey in everyday language why dogs behave a certain way in certain situations and how you can use this knowledge to make life with your dog as rewarding as possible.

Behavior Patterns of Dogs

The behavior patterns of a dog are determined by the animal's basic nature, which, in spite of the long association with humans still retains many wolf qualities:
- Dogs are predators and therefore suited for hunting.
- They have very strong territorial instincts, which is why they make good watchdogs.
- Their social behavior, which derives from their originally living in packs, makes dogs such good companions.

To this heritage of their ancestors, dogs have in the course of living with humans added an intelligence that is based on the ability to remember past experiences. With the help of this intelligence, dogs can learn to vary their behavior to suit different occasions.

There are two very different principles at work that we have to be able to distinguish:

1. Certain reactions (such as the reaction to the visual perception of movement) are almost entirely automatic processes.

2. At the same time a dog is an autonomous, highly sensitive creature that makes conscious decisions.

The behavior of a dog is a combination of
- inborn behavior patterns belonging to the species dog;

- specific behavior patterns characteristic of the particular breed;
- learned behavior acquired through training and coexistence with humans;
- expression of feelings and emotional associations that also derive from close association with humans.

For a dog that is attached to people, expression of affection or praise is just as important as a concrete reward such as a dog biscuit. For dogs are no strangers to feelings like love, envy, or jealousy. In Eric H. W. Aldington's book *About the Souls of Dogs* I found the following illustration:

Jealous Pete

Pete had always hated being brushed—perhaps he was ticklish. In any case he always tried to get the part of himself that was about to be brushed out of the brush's reach and developed a great facility at this. Then a new small dog joined the household: Henry loved to be brushed. Pete did not watch idly for long. By way of a chair he climbed up on the table, stood over Henry crosswise, and stared at his master mutely. "Moved, I put the little dog back on the floor and started working on Pete, who let himself be brushed with uncharacteristic patience, politeness, and satisfaction, while below Henry was jumping around the table, yapping furiously."

Special Behavioral Traits of Different Breeds

Selective breeding by humans has made some dog breeds "difficult to read," but at the same time selective breeding has also fostered certain qualities and types of behavior that make it possible to describe the typical character of different breeds (see Breeds, pages 128–166). How, for instance, are you going to interpret the facial expression of an Old English sheepdog that hides behind a thick mop of hair, or the expression of a Doberman or a bullterrier, whose skin is stretched so tight across the face that hardly a muscle can move (giving these dogs what people tend to call an "insincere" look); what are you to make of a basset whose skin folds parody feelings that aren't there at all?

Character traits and behavior patterns are inherited. Fox terriers are exceptionally lively. Shown here is a wirehaired fox terrier with a nine-week-old puppy.

Pugs have long been underappreciated and have a reputation of being surly. In fact, they are pleasant and cheerful dogs.

As far as personality goes, breeds like Pyrenean sheepdogs or sled dogs, terriers, and dachshunds are decidedly strong-willed and need to be trained with a firm hand. They will try again and again to improve their rank position in the family hierarchy. You don't have to worry about this with hunting dogs like beagles and bassets. They, like poodles and greyhounds, accept human authority unquestioningly. Different breeds have repeatedly been studied in the context of family life (that is, not under laboratory conditions) to analyze their inherent behavior, and the results of these observations should be taken into account by prospective dog owners who are about to choose a breed.

A United States Survey Rates Different Breeds as Follows:

Easy to train: Doberman pinschers, Welsh corgis, miniature poodles, and toy poodles

Hard to train: Basset hounds, dachshunds, fox terriers, dalmatians, and Pekinese

Especially lively: Fox terriers, West Highland white terriers, schnauzers, and Yorkshire terriers

Notable for being quiet: Bloodhounds, basset hounds, Newfoundlands, Australian shepherd dogs

Exceptionally good watchdogs: Schnauzers, West Highland white terriers, Scottish terriers, Dobermans, German shepherd dogs

Less good watchdogs: Bloodhounds, Newfoundlands, Saint Bernards, basset hounds, vizsla

Don't like children: Miniature schnauzers, dachshunds, Afghans, sheepdogs

Put up with children: Dalmatians, giant schnauzers, standard schnauzers, collies, Hovawarts, Dobermans, and Bernese mountain dogs

Love children: Bulldogs, bullterriers, Great Danes, boxers, rottweilers, and Newfoundlands.

A personal observation: There are individual dogs that are the exact opposite of how the list classifies them. That is one of the disadvantages of generalizations based on observation and speaks strongly for the individuality of dogs. Although it may be hard for us with some breeds to tell their facial expression (see page 55), it is nevertheless a fact that dogs communicate with their faces most of the time, as well as with their ears, their fur, and their tails (see Body Lanugage, page 57). Here I can't help but observe that docking tails and/or cropping ears is a barbarous practice that deprives dogs of some important means of communication (see Glossary, DOCKING AND CROPPING).

Tail-wagging Expresses Different Moods

Even people who know nothing about dogs can tell you that a dog that wags its tail is a friendly dog. That much is common knowledge. But not everybody knows that tail wagging is a highly differentiated mode of expression that can indicate a whole range of moods. How is a poor boxer with the tiny stub of tail it has left after docking to let us know whether it is happy, friendly, excited, or in a state of conflicting emotions? Dogs use their tails to communicate with people as well as with other dogs.

A furiously wagging tail indicates friendly feelings toward either a person or a dog. My male basset hounds have a special circular wag for females of their species; the tail rotates like a propeller to express intense interest.

A slow, brief wagging, sometimes merely a few thumps on the floor if the dog is lying down, expresses the dog's fondness for the person to whom the wagging is addressed.

A raised tail that moves back and forth slowly like the windshield wipers of a car expresses a potentially dangerous conflict between wanting to greet and wanting to challenge a person or another dog. The dog doesn't know yet what to do.

A tail between the legs means restraint or fear.

A tail carried horizontally is a sign of great contentment.

Watch your dog for other messages of tail wagging. You learn to understand dog language only through close observation.

A Dog Has Two Languages

One language is for dealing with dogs, the other for communicating with people. The two overlap in part, and only the nose and scent language (see A Dog's Nose, page 49) is closed to us. Dog language also includes barking (see Vocal language, page 62). Body language is expressed in posture and gestures, both of which involve the entire body, including tail, ears, face, and fur. Even dogs that are completely integrated into the human world should still be able to communicate with their own kind, although they may not really need this ability in their daily lives.

A dog that no longer knows the rules that regulate canine interaction is not a real dog anymore, and walks with it are difficult because the dog is uncertain how to behave toward other four-legged, fur-bearing and tail-bearing creatures. Such a dog is likely to respond with ambivalence

Akita puppies at play. The one on the ground seems to be acting out the gesture of subordination.

Every meeting between dogs begins with nose contact. Here a cocker spaniel and a six-week-old Old English sheepdog pup are going through the first stage of mutual investigation. Notice the tense posture of the spaniel.

or timidity, stay away from other dogs altogether, or overcompensate by trying to pick fights.

How Dogs Get Acquainted: Nose Contact

What happens when two dogs meet? They introduce themselves with their noses. You can see it over and over: Two dogs meet for the first time. They walk up to each other, nose up front, until they almost touch. Then they sniff each other to find out how they like each other. After this initial scent check, a friendly or unfriendly relationship develops. Ethologists call this greeting "nose contact."

For this process of getting acquainted to function properly both dogs must be normal, not neurotic, and they must have a normal attitude toward other dogs.

Whether or not this is so depends on you, the dogs' owners. If you have always picked up your puppy as soon as another dog approached, if you have kept your dog away from other dogs and stopped any

contact that might have developed, don't be surprised if your dog now avoids contact with other dogs. These are the dogs that whine and try to get away from nose contact and sniffing or that yap and growl and try to hurl themselves at any dog they glimpse. They are either terrible cowards when confronted with another dog or they are carried away by a false feeling of superiority that blinds them to reality, so that a dachshund may attack a German shepherd dog. In spite of all the affection their families may lavish on them they remain outsiders, because contact between dogs is an essential part of being a dog. All dog owners should get their dogs used to dog encounters from early puppyhood so that the dogs can learn the rules of proper conduct. It's perfectly safe to let a puppy approach any dog. No grown dog, no matter how overbred, forgets the natural law that says: "Never bite the young of your species."

Dr. Dorit Feddersen-Petersen, an ethologist, does say that poodles have lost the ability to communicate with or

even understand other dogs. In the breeding of poodles, it was always the individuals that related best with humans that were selected for reproduction. Nobody cared how they got along with other dogs, and so the wolflike qualities were gradually bred out while those making the dogs good human companions were strengthened, with the result that poodles now care only about contact with their humans.

Rules Dominating Dog Encounters

Like everything in the world of dogs, encounters are regulated by strict rules.

Once two dogs have had nose contact, they either have to wag their tails next time they meet—which means something like "Hello there, friend"—or they have to growl, which can be translated as "Keep your distance!" A dog knows whether or not it has met this particular dog before because of its excellent memory for scents. You'll be able to tell easily enough whether or not your dog likes the other one, but there is not much you can do about it. And you will never know the reasons for the like or dislike.

Very assertive or very large dogs have a third option. They can ignore certain dogs, walking past them as though they didn't exist.

Smelling the rear end is the second stage of nose contact. This anal check is by no means disgusting but is quite natural, because the glands that tell dogs what they want to know about each other are located underneath the tail. Scientists call this zone the "anal face" (see Glossary, ANAL FACE), and dogs that display this face with raised tail to any other dog, naturally and unabashedly, are self-confident dogs.

It depends on the relative rank position of the dogs which dog is allowed to sniff the other. For rank (social hierarchy) plays a crucial role with dogs. A hierarchy is in force not only among dogs that live together but also at chance encounters. In the dog world as in human life, there are dominant types and permanent "underdogs." Battles are fought to determine

The next phase in the process of getting acquainted: the anal check. The dogs in the picture are mongrels.

Big dogs usually rank higher than little dogs in the social hierarchy. The dog in the picture is a black giant schnauzer.

which dog ranks above the other. How can you recognize in good time when a fight is in the making? Assuming that both dogs are behaving normally and naturally, this is how the encounter will go:

From Dog Encounter to Dog Fight

After nose contact, the dogs stand parallel to each other and sniff each other's behind. As long as the tails wag happily there's nothing to worry about.

Timid dogs get all stiff during such a meeting, and the hair on their back stands on end. This is a sign of insecurity and doesn't necessarily indicate a readiness to fight. The more self-assured the other dog is, the more harmless the situation.

If both dogs feel about equally bold and one of them stops wagging its tail, the other one, too, will let its tail go stiff and raise its fur, thus signaling: "I'm not going to put up with that." Then both start circling each other slowly, bumping each other with the shoulder. If one of them now lowers the tail, thus covering the anal

region, this means "I don't want any trouble," and the crisis has passed. The other is accepted as higher ranking, and this may even be the beginning of a friendship.

If neither is willing to give in and they change their positions to form a T—one is standing crosswise in front of the other—a fight may erupt, with the dog that forms the horizontal bar of the T defending itself and the one forming the vertical bar acting as aggressor.

At this point it is still possible to avert the fight—but not by yanking your dog away from the other one. This is more likely to trigger an immediate outbreak of hostilities. Neither dog should be made to lose face; if one of them does, it will attack any nearby dog, innocent or not, to vent its anger. Try to separate the dogs by giving a firm command—for example, "Fido, come!" or, simply, "No!" Often the "higher authority" of the master is a good excuse to terminate the affair nonviolently. Distract the dogs' attention from each other; the situation and the level of your dog's obedience will determine how you go about it.

If you have missed the opportunity to separate the dogs in time, a fight may be unavoidable. But no matter how terrifying a dog fight may look, it is usually not too serious. However, this is true only if both dogs have learned how to deal with other dogs and if they observe the basic laws of dog behavior. Uncontrolled biting by dogs with weakened natural instincts can leave the contestants quite bloody. But the noisier a fight, the more harmless it really is. The only injuries that are likely to result from it are on the lips, if the dogs's teeth clash.

If one dog subordinates itself or gives in, the conflict is over. This is assuming that both dogs' instincts are intact. I am deliberately not giving rules on how to break up a dog fight the way people used to. Individual dogs and situations vary too much to allow generalizations. Dog owners can terminate a fight only if both dogs are pulled back simultaneously. The best way is to "pull the rug from under their feet"

by picking them up. But in trying to do this you may well get bitten by your darling. If this should happen, don't blame the dog and carry a grudge. Dogs are as though in a trance when they fight—they hear nothing; they feel nothing; they are aware only of their opponent.

Dogs on a leash get into fights much more often than dogs that are used to meeting others of their kind by themselves. The leash is like an extension of the master's arm and makes a dog feel twice as bold as it would be otherwise. But knowing this is of little help if leash laws continue to be extended to public parks— which is where most dogs get a chance to meet each other.

Encounters between two male dogs always end with both of them lifting a leg. This is part of canine ritual and enhances each dog's sense of self-worth. You should let your dog engage in this ritual even on the leash.

Two bitches should always be kept at a safe distance from each other. If they get into a tussle they are bound by no rules

The running capacity of basset hounds is usually underestimated. These dogs can run fast and for a long time without tiring.

Leaping into the water. Most dogs love the water and know instinctively how to swim.

and fight brutally. If you are in a park where there are many dogs, try to ascertain in advance by calling out from a distance to ask whether an approaching dog is a male or a female. And don't let your dog off the leash unless you are prepared for an encounter.

A bitch only rarely allows a male to check her anal region.

Principles Governing Contact Between Dogs

1. The more dogs a dog knows, the more relaxed and natural is its behavior.
2. Dogs don't resort to their teeth instantly; first they threaten and pretend.
3. There are breeds that show little interest in other dogs. Among these are fox terriers and bullterriers. They should be left alone.
4. There is nothing more wonderful than friendships between dogs. Half an hour of playing together provides as much exercise as a two-hour walk.

The Vocal Language of Dogs

"What does the dog say?" is a command that some owners use to get their dogs to bark. For humans, the vocal utterances of dogs, culminating in barking, are synonymous with dog language. I have jotted down over a period of time all the kinds of sounds my dogs produce.

Here is the repertoire of their utterances: They bark, yelp, give tongue, yap, growl, yodel, wail, howl, bay, squeal, roar, cry, whimper, whine, squeak, grunt, and mutter. There are also mixtures and combinations of these sounds, for which I have no words. This list is limited to sounds used to communicate; it does not contain expressions of pain.

To learn to understand your dog: A dog can squeal in excited anticipation or cry with fear; it can whine out of boredom or squeak before falling asleep. You have to learn to interpret this sound language along with the body language. If, for instance, your dachshund greets you, beside itself with joy, wagging not only the tail

but the entire posterior half, curling the body first to one side and then the other, bouncing up and down like a rubber ball, yodeling and barking until your ears are ringing, this is a greeting that requires an answer. All you need to say is: "It's okaaaay, you're a goooood doooog," and the dog will calm down. If, on the other hand, your dog produces a monotonous series of "woof-woofs," looks at you intently, and wags its tail vigorously back and forth, it's time for a walk. A loud, persistent "woww-woww" can mean "Where is my food?" and a low growl combined with raised fur and a short bark indicates that there is someone at the door ready to ring the bell, while an excited "Wo-wo-wo-wouff" announces that the bell has been rung.

Important: the human reaction. Dog lovers understand every sound their dogs make and respond appropriately. This is part of a good relationship between dog and human. Responding appropriately means maintaining a good balance between disregarding and picking up on the dog's suggestions. A dog owner who is too responsive and obedient soon becomes the dog's servant, a situation any dog recognizes instantly and exploits shamelessly.

Barking: Among the many dogs I have come to know there are babblers, silent ones, noise boxes, and ones that speak with deliberation. There are dogs that bark with uninhibited enjoyment, comparable to people who like telling you what they think about everything. In a large park with many dogs I can tell the different kinds of dogs that are barking nearby and farther away: Boxers and other dogs with massive heads have gruff voices that sound as though they were talking with their mouths full. Dalmatians and setters produce melodiously yodeling songs, and collies monotonously keep saying the same thing over. If you listen critically you could say that barking is less like uttered speech than like moods set to music. Barking is a skill dogs did not develop until they started living with humans and have since perfected to a fine art.

Important for daily living: The better you are at interpreting your dog's barking and *the more you respond to it*, the more the dog will bark.

With hunting breeds (see Glossary, hunting dogs) the dogs' barking is cultivated so that they can inform the hunter of things that only dogs with their more acute sense organs can detect. The hunting dog's bark takes on different tones when it is following a scent; when it catches sight of the game; when the quarry is wounded, treed, or cornered; and when the animal is dead.

And what about the saying "Barking dogs don't bite"? A dog that barks doesn't need to bite. It warns of a stranger's approach and thus drives the stranger away. And besides, a dog that is barking is rarely in a biting mood. If a dog wants to bite, it does so quickly and silently.

How Humans Talk with Their Dogs

When your dog barks you respond with words, your hands, and gestures of affection (see page 65). To be able to talk with your dog you have to get over your embarrassment first, for many people feel foolish and inhibited when they try to utter the cheerful and affectionate nonsense that dogs love so much. Try to overcome your self-consciousness and say, without human witnesses at first, "Yeees, you're a goood wonnderful looovely Suzy-dooog." Keep in mind that barking has an emotional dimension and try to be just as emotional when you talk your own private dog talk. What matters is not the meaning of the words but the singsong quality of your voice, its pitch, and the soothing tone. Your dog will love it.

How effective such talk can be was proven to me one day when a Doberman pinscher decided to block my path. My most entreating "Move!" and my most assertive "Get away!" were equally ineffective. The Doberman pretended not to hear. I decided to shift gears, tried to make eye contact with a smile, and then said "My goood fiiine dumbbell Doberman-dooog." The dog wagged its tail briefly and, after

Every fourth dog owner has a mongrel. The dog on the left in the picture is a mixture of German shepherd dog and dachshund; the one on the right is a German shepherd and rottweiler mix.

lifting a leg, took off for the bushes. From that moment on I've been a convinced believer in praise and friendliness to achieve good relations between humans and canines.

Note: The most important thing in trying to make eye contact with a dog is the smile, creating an aura of good will. Otherwise looking at the dog intently will be interpreted as a threat.

Gestures of Affection

Since we lack two important means of communication—we have neither a tail for wagging nor ears that can be pricked up or flattened—we supplement vocal utterances with gestures to demonstrate our fondness. We pet the dog, but not the same way one pets a cat to make it purr, by stroking it with the flat of the hand in the direction in which the fur grows. Dogs don't like this so much; they prefer to be scratched.

I distinguish six different ways of showing physical affection to a dog:

1. Scratching the chest, which male dogs like particularly.

2. Scratching just above the tail; this makes most dogs ecstatic.

3. Scratching under the chin gently with the tips of your fingers.

4. Rubbing the ears and scratching just behind the ears.

5. Light tapping and petting on the back—but, please, not the equivalent of slapping someone on the back.

6. Placing the flat of your hand on the dog's back or belly and letting it rest there for a while.

If the dog reciprocates by licking your hand, please don't pull the hand away and scold the dog, but let it do as it wishes. You can wash your hands afterwards.

From Dog to Dog: How Dogs Communicate Their Feelings

Dogs have very subtle methods of telling each other how they feel. They do it with their whole bodies, their tails, ears, and the fur. When a dog, filled with anticipatory excitement, moves toward something, every part of it is focused and upright: the body, the ears, the neck, and the tail. The dog is making itself look as big as it can. The increased size is supposed to frighten the other dog; the posture of attentiveness turns into a posture of threatening. Students of animal behavior call this "intimidation display."

Intimidation behavior involves baring the teeth without necessarily intending to use them, and making oneself look bigger by raising the fur, lifting the head, pricking the ears, walking on stiff legs, holding the tail rigid and sometimes straight up in the air like a flagpole. All this is done while standing broadside to the challenger's head and staring at him (see Glossary, INTIMIDATION DISPLAY). Such an encounter can determine the ranking order of two dogs without recourse to a fight.

Here is a point for you to ponder. If size is so important and threatening to dogs, how must we appear to them? Depending on a dog's breed we are anywhere from two to six times the animal's size. That is the reason I urge you not to consciously use your height to intimidate a dog. With dominant dogs, on the other hand, your size may be what saves you. Biting incidents occur almost exclusively if a person falls down and loses the advantage of height.

Defensive behavior: This is the opposite of intimidating behavior. The dog is reluctant to move toward something and lowers everything—the head, the ears, the tail—and flattens its fur. These reactions are not meant as a threat; the dog wants only to make its escape as quickly as possible.

What a Dog's Ears Tell Us

The most obvious indicator of a dog's moods and intentions are its ears, especially if the dog has natural prick ears, though even a spaniel or a basset hound with its long, drooping ears can still convey quite a bit with them. In a sweeping generalization we can say that

- *ears standing straight up* indicate watchfulness, attention, and self-confidence;

- *ears pointed forward or turned side-*

ways signal readiness to attack;

- *ears flattened or folded back* are a sign of insecurity.

If a dog barks with ears pricked up while wagging its tail at the same time, this is a sign of conflicting emotions. This behavior is quite common in dogs behind a fence. They want to defend their territory but at the same time they would like to make friends. It's impossible to predict which feeling will triumph; even the dog doesn't know at that moment.

As a general rule we can say:

- The more self-confident a dog is, the more actively its tail will wag back and forth.
- If the tail is held rigid and stiff, we are dealing with a reserved, cautious dog that may even be afraid. This kind of dog may bite out of fear.
- Dogs that hold their tails between their legs tend to belong to the class of underdogs, except for the greyhound breeds, which have been deliberately bred to keep their tails between the legs all the time.

We have already discussed what tail-wagging means (see page 56). Just be sure not to mistake the twitching back and forth of a raised tail for tail wagging. A raised tail means that excited attention is focused on something in front of the dog. Here you have to rely on the facial expression for clues. A mean expression and a raised tail in motion means: Watch out! Another sign of this mood is the raised fur, especially near the root of the tail.

How a Dog Communicates through Its Fur

Dogs have inherited from their wolf ancestors the capacity to raise some parts of their fur at will. This is most obviously seen in the area near the base of the tail. If the fur stands up there, the animal is trying to tell me: "This far but no closer!" A step closer elicits a low growl. I've never tried to find out what would happen next. Wolves also have the ability to raise the fur on their faces and can turn them into scary masks.

Fur standing on end and a raised tail go together in one threatening gesture. If the tail droops to body level, the overall threatening image is ruined: The dog is no longer sure of itself.

When the fur is flattened, the entire dog seems to lose size, and everything points downward. The dog is giving up. It would like best to slink away. It may even lie down and roll on its back in a gesture of submission.

When Dogs Laugh

Among my acquaintances there are some who assure me that their dogs laugh—or, in any event, smile. I never doubt these reports, and the only thing that amazes me is that people seem to consider it so special. Many people seem to think their dog is the only one to laugh or that only some breeds, such as borzois, do it. Laughing is not so rare in dogs. When a dog stretches its lips, raises the corners of the mouth, and opens its jaws slightly, it is making a playful face; the expression is comparable to a human smile. Since dogs don't bare their teeth when they smile, there is no fear of mistaking the smile for a threatening expression. Dogs put on this "laughing" face both with humans and with other dogs.

Smell As a Means of Communication

I said earlier that "dogs see the world through their noses." By this I mean that dogs have a nose or scent language that is closed to us, and I have alluded to this language in my discussion of dog encounters (see page 58). You can observe it every day on your dog walks when your dog sniffs everything and, if it is a male, has to lift its leg. That the dog is literally compelled to do so is perfectly obvious to any dog lover or dog expert. Some environmentalists think that this constant sprinkling of urine on trees, fences, and corners of buildings is harmful and prevents the affected plants from thriving. But to forbid a dog to lift its leg would be to forbid the expression of inborn needs.

When a male dog lifts its leg it is not just to empty its bladder. The main purpose of the action is to leave scent signals for other dogs. The dog dispenses its urine

Opposite page: "Like cat and dog?" Contrary to long-standing folklore, friendships between cats and dogs are quite common. In the picture a female Hovawart is posing with a house cat.

in carefully measured doses. Students of animal behavior speak of "scent marks," because the dog is defining the borders of its territory with its urine and announcing those borders to the noses of all other dogs. Outside its own territory the dog leaves messages saying "I was here," and whichever dog can lift its leg the highest is the greatest.

The Best Marker on the Block?

Fax was a hunting terrier. He was endowed with good looks and an ego to more than match his looks. Most of the time he walked with a spring to his gait as though he could hardly contain his own power. When he lifted his leg, he turned into a circus acrobat. No other dog's scent mark was so high that he could not top it. If a big dog had passed by before him, he balanced on two legs, and if need be he walked his hind legs up the wall to aim his squirt at just the right spot. There was no doubt about it: He was the best marker far and wide.

Why Dogs Sniff and Smell

Dogs sniff and smell the way people look around the world or read the paper. It's a dog's way to experience the world in its manifold scent manifestations, and every hint of a smell bears information. If there are traces of urine smell, a male dog is compelled to cover them up with its own marks. By the way, there are dominant bitches that do the same. (Normally females don't use their urine to leave scent marks but void the entire bladder at once and squat to do so.) Dogs prefer to leave their marks where others have done so before. This collecting and leaving of scent messages is very important to all dogs, but particularly to males. If you prevent your dog from engaging in this behavior you are—to overstate the case somewhat—guilty of mental cruelty.

Dogs appreciate smells we would just as soon pretend didn't exist. And since they have such good noses, they detect even the slightest whiffs. Don't be surprised or embarrassed if a dog sticks its nose under your skirt or sniffs the back of your pants. For a dog, human beings are surrounded by a cloud of smells from which the dog picks out its favorite perfumes. This, too, is a form of communication and contact.

About Digging and Pawing

Burying bones and leftover meat is an ancient habit that dogs inherited from their past as wolves and that originally had the purpose of letting the meat cure and of laying in provisions for leaner times. Dogs still persist in this habit, even though living with humans eliminates the need for food reserves. Dogs still like to bury bits of food and occasionally a toy in the garden. After depositing the item to be saved, a dog pushes the loose earth around with its nose to cover up the hole. You can observe the same motions indoors (pawing the floor) when your dog tries to "bury" something there.

The Sex Drive in Dogs

This is a rather sad chapter, especially for male dogs, because their sexual drives are not limited to certain seasons, as they are in females (see Glossary, ESTRUS), but assert themselves all year round. Some people say that 90 percent of all dogs living in cities suffer from psychological disorders caused by sexual frustration.

Surrogate Behavior Arising from Sexual Frustration?

Sometimes dogs regard their humans as sexual partners and try to make love to them, or they mount young or other lower-ranking males.

A dog mounting another dog is a surrogate action and has nothing to do with sodomy or homosexuality. It is an unsuccessful attempt on the part of the dog to relieve its sexual misery.

Dog embracing a human leg can be embarrassing. A dog latches on to a person's leg with its front legs and executes powerful thrusts with its pelvis. Dogs like human legs not only because we seem like close partners to them but also because legs are easier to get hold of than pillows. You should not get upset if your dog engages in such surrogate behavior, but instead feel sorry for it. Harsh punishment is not in order; usually a reprimand is all that is needed. Of course, if a domineering dog tries to assert its superiority over you by clutching your leg, this is insolence and must be stopped immediately. I once knew a woman who had a dachshund that hung onto her leg most of the time and refused to budge even when she crossed the room.

When Male Dogs Catch the Scent of a Bitch in Heat

This is a situation that arouses male dogs to a high pitch. The following are unmistakable signs that a male is smelling the urine of a female in heat: He sniffs the spot repeatedly, then keeps raising his head and staring into the distance with silent concentration; then he rattles his teeth. This means that the chemical message is very powerful. Now is the time to have a firm hold of the leash, for even the best behaved and tamest dog will try under

these circumstances to make a dash for the unknown beauty.

In the spring, when the heat periods of bitches living close by and within a wider radius coincide, the males are in a frenzy. They become restless and try desperately to get to one of the females. They dig their way under fences, jump or climb over them, make a dash for freedom as soon as the front door opens, run away while on a walk—all things they wouldn't dream of doing normally. Or they wail their love songs with open mouths, their heads thrown back, and the front feet sometimes rising off the ground.

A Word of Advice to Owners of Female Dogs

If you don't want to give your bitch heat-suppressant hormone treatments (see page 100), it is best for your dog to keep as low a profile as possible. This means: Carry your dog out of the house, or drive her by car, to a spot inaccessible to male dogs, where she can relieve herself. Only if there is no direct line of scent leading to

A mother dog nurses her pups for about four to six weeks. Shown is an Irish setter bitch with her three-week-old litter.

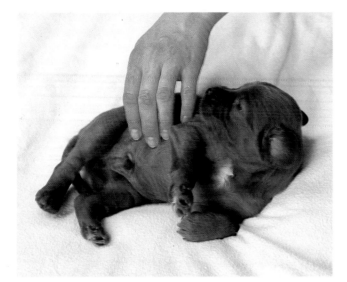

Checking the puppy's sex also means physical contact between puppy and human being. A puppy begins to establish its first bond to humans at three to seven weeks. The puppy in the picture is a three-week-old Irish setter.

overpopulation of canines. Every one of us has a role in making sure that dog breeding be done conscientiously and consequently within strict limits. If an unplanned mating takes place, you can take your female dog to the veterinarian four to six days after the "mistake" for an injection that will terminate the pregnancy. If you don't want to do this, your dog will give birth after about 60 days, though the puppies quite often arrive before the due date. Discuss the birth process with your veterinarian or someone who has experience in this area, and get some literature on the topic (see Bibliography, page 170).

Please also read the Glossary entries, ESTRUS and FALSE PREGNANCY.

Pregnancy and Birth

If a mating has resulted in pregnancy, the veterinarian or an experienced breeder can first feel the fetuses between the 22nd and 28th day. After five weeks the dog's belly begins to swell. The birth usually takes place 60 to 63 days after mating, most frequently—according to statistics—around 3 A.M

Make sure that

- the dog is not exposed to hardship during the pregnancy;
- it gets especially nutritious food;
- you prepare the whelping box in good time;
- you get the dog used to the place where it will give birth.

You have to decide for yourself whether you feel comfortable attending the birth without outside help. About 24 hours before labor pains set in, the dog begins to get restless. When the pains start it may still be hours before the puppies are born. You have to remain very calm during this time. This is important for your dog's sake, for animals sense if you feel panicked. The first puppy takes the longest to emerge, but as long as the mother stays calm the birth will proceed normally. There may be anywhere between four (toy poodles) and eight (Saint Bernards) puppies in a litter. Beagles, too, tend to have large litters. I can't give you instructions on complicated births because I have no experience here.

your house can you hope to keep your front door from being besieged by amorous males.

Letting a bitch run free when she is in heat is most inconsiderate. Not only will she, too, take off on her own sooner or later, but you are forcing owners—panting along on the other end of the leash—to retrace the erratic course the bitch took. But I know owners of bitches who do let their dog run free, and call out to people with male dogs to please put them on the leash because their bitch is in heat. Owners of male dogs who refuse to cooperate in such a situation have my full sympathy.

If two dogs manage to copulate, they remain hooked together for about 15 minutes. Any attempt to try to separate them by force is brutal and can lead to serious injuries in both dogs.

Motherhood

My account of the events connected with motherhood is not meant as a set of instructions for amateur breeders to follow. I simply want to describe for you, a dog owner, the pregnancy of a dog and the birth of puppies. There are absolutely no health reasons why a female dog should have puppies, and I beg you to see to it that your dog does not contribute to the

Dogs—Best Medicine for Humans

Doctors, psychologists, and sociologists have discovered that dogs, our most faithful pets, not only guard homes and make good companions, but also serve a health-promoting function. Dogs improve the physical and emotional well-being of their owners.

- Many doctors recommend getting a dog as a long-term therapy against lack of exercise and the medical problems arising from this lack.
- Physicians and psychologists also agree that a dog is the best cure for stress associated with work.
- Dogs are even more important in people's lives after retirement. A dog not only gives a person the feeling of still being needed but also requires daily care and provides occasion for contact with others. This is particularly important in a time of isolation and retirement from work life.

A Dog as a Means to Get Exercise

Lack of exercise is responsible for various forms of physical decline that can lead to actual illness. The simplest form of exercise, walking, can counteract the process of physical deterioration. When asked if walking contributes to a higher life expectancy, 85 out of 100 doctors responded with a clear yes. Anyone owning a dog has to walk regularly, and half of all dog owners spend 10 to 20 hours a week walking with their dogs. Walking this much keeps you healthy.

A Dog as Healer

Regular walks like this can also be used in rehabilitation situations. Erika Friedmann, an American university professor, studied patients who had suffered heart attacks and found that the rate of survival was four times greater for owners of pets than for people without pets. She came to the conclusion not only that the increased physical activity provided by a dog has a life-prolonging effect, but also that a dog's companionship and need for care are of direct physiological benefit.

A handful of dog: This four-day-old puppy will grow into a strong Entlebucher mountain dog—a breed that is little known outside of its native Switzerland.

A Dog at the Sickbed

Nursing homes in the United States and in Australia have found that when they suspend the standard rule against allowing pets, the constant contact with their own dogs is a positive and life-affirming experience for old people.

In Germany, Professor Wolfgang Piotrovski, Director of the Neurosurgical Clinic of Mannheim, is a proponent of this kind of therapy. He is convinced that dogs and patients living together has a soothing effect on the patients and recommends the presence of dogs especially in radiation therapy centers and in follow-up clinics for cancer patients. He suggests dachshunds, poodles, and schnauzers as candidates to serve as "dogs in the sickroom." The problem of hygiene (see also page 103), which of course has to be considered, would not be insurmountable.

A Dog as Enhancer of Psychological Well-being

A dog can clearly enhance the quality of life for humans.

It can fill central psychological needs by, for instance, dispelling loneliness and boredom, facilitating social contact, and providing opportunities to feel appreciated and understood.

It also gives its owner a positive self image, an acceptance of self, and increased self-confidence.

A Dog as an Aid for Coping with Life

It is the opinion of most psychotherapists that dogs are ideal companions for people who suffer from certain mental illnesses or nervous disorders. Dr. Marcel Heimann of Mount Sinai Hospital in New York explains it like this: "For mental patients, a dog is often the anchor that keeps them from slipping all the way into the disease. By taking care of a dog, a self-absorbed person can learn to place another creature's needs above his or her own wishes. A dog also provides an outlet for pent-up feelings of love in people who for some reason can no longer express this love toward other human beings."

Dogs provide an important relationship for people who are under stress though not yet sick or who are going through difficult times. Contact with a dog relieves negative feelings. Anxiety can be reduced by petting a dog, and the physical contact can even lower blood pressure.

A Dog as an Aid for Prolonging Life

For older people there is hardly a better method for staying healthy and cheerful than to live with a dog. A dog is often the last, thin wall that keeps a lonely old person from depression and giving up.

A dog can be of great help to the physically handicapped. Here a German shepherd/ rottweiler mix that is certified to conduct itself properly in traffic is accompanying a person in a motorized wheelchair.

Teaching a Dog to Be a Pleasant Companion

There are many books on training dogs, recommending many views and approaches. In this guide I devote only a few pages to this subject, which will nonetheless, I hope, be of use to you. I restrict myself to only the most important commands, which, however, should be thoroughly mastered.

Basic Course for the Trainer

An important rule for training dogs is: The earlier you start working with your dog, the easier it will be to teach. The first experiences a dog has with humans are crucial for the rest of its life.

There Has to Be Authority!

If you believe in antiauthoritarian education for children, forget these theories for dog training. When dealing with humans, the secret of success is to get along with each other, to be friendly and tolerant toward others, and to be able to give in now and then. In teaching dogs, authority is the secret of success. If you fail to provide authority, the dog does as it pleases and starts acting up: It stops obeying altogether. Don't worry: Your dog won't stop loving you even if it no longer accepts your authority; it just doesn't respect you the same way anymore. By authority I don't mean the kind of power that rules by fear, but the unquestioned superiority of a leader whose decisions

consistently require obedience. To be successful in this role requires a mixture of loving empathy and determined discipline—discipline, however, that is most effectively expressed through praise.

The Principles of Training a Dog

1. Teach your dog no more than necessary but be very exact and exacting in what you do teach.
2. Teach your dog everything it needs for a happy coexistence, including coexistence with your neighbors.
3. Before you start practicing with your dog, practice first by yourself. Teaching a dog requires some qualities that you might not pay much attention to in day-to-day life (see page 74).
4. The practice sessions should become a kind of ritual for your dog. When you practice with your dog, be methodical, precise, and insistent on minute observation of your commands, even if that's not the way you generally are. Generous laxity is not useful in this training course, no matter how intelligent your dog may be.

Qualities a Dog Trainer Has to Have

During all the training exercises a friendly atmosphere should prevail. That is why a dog trainer not only needs to exude authority but should also have the following qualities:

Lots of patience: No matter how obtuse or easily distracted your dog is, you should never lose your temper or get discouraged. Even if your dog shows no interest in learning, you must retain and show your enthusiasm for each exercise.

Firmness: Repeat each exercise until it is thoroughly mastered. Never let the dog decide when to stop; you are the one to determine when a lesson is over. Keep going over the same exercises; later they become part of the practice ritual. You must never allow yourself to get bored during practice.

Good humor: Training a dog is not a matter of intimidation or threats. The mood during the practice sessions should be relaxed and friendly; this does not mean letting the dog get away with things. Perhaps friendly strictness is the right phrase for it.

Staying relaxed: Don't put yourself under pressure, and don't set yourself a time limit by when an exercise should be mastered. The more relaxed and calm you are when you work with your dog, the better the lessons go. Avoid tension that could make your dog nervous.

Honest self-assessment: This begins with the selection of the dog's breed. Does your dog really fit you or is it "one size too big"? It is, of course, possible to progress by overcoming initial difficulties. The terms "complementary dog" and "resonance dog" indicate only a general idea, but they might be of some help in deciding on a breed. A complementary dog is one whose qualities complete or balance those of its owner's temperament. An even-tempered dog, for instance, would be good for a hotheaded person, and a lively dog would be the answer for an apathetic person. A resonance dog is one that is on the same wavelength as its owner: An active and cheerful dog would be a good match for an optimist, and a calm, subdued canine would fit a melancholy personality.

Train your voice, almost as though you wanted to become an actor. Keep practicing until you can express a command, praise, or rebuke in a tone that the dog can understand. It is by the voice that a dog can tell if its owner means what has

The more you teach a puppy, the easier life together will be later on. This trio of eight-week-old English bulldog puppies are ready for their first lessons.

been said and if the dog has pleased or displeased. Since the hearing of dogs is very good you don't need to yell; it's the tone of voice that matters. Keep using the same simple words, and make sure you know which words you want to use. Words are the keys to your dog's brain; they trigger the process of reactions that we call obedience. And don't talk too much during the lessons. Let your voice ring and sing only when you praise.

Control of your movements: Watch yourself in a mirror when you work with your dog, or—better yet, though more expensive—have someone videotape a training session. Are you in control of your body, your arms, your hands? Or are you flapping and floundering? Dogs are geniuses at understanding body language. The accomplishments of circus dogs are based on their ability to react to the most inconspicuous signals. Only if body language and spoken commands are at odds with each other does a dog get confused. Get used to making an appropriate gesture with each command, such as a downward motion with your flat hand to accompany the word "Sit!" or a beckoning wave when you call "Come!"

The Talents and Traits of Domestic Dogs

To learn through play, that is a great secret of success that all social beings share. Dogs love to learn. Nature has endowed them with talents and traits that make it easy for them to learn to obey; this accounts for the fact that dogs have become our most popular pets. Some of these talents and traits are

- the pack instinct, which consists of an overwhelming desire to be part of a group;
- a readiness to subordinate oneself. This is essential for successful coexistence in a group. Dogs, which have remained wolf-like in this respect, first subordinate themselves to the male parent and later to the leader of the pack. You, as the dog's master, are taking over this leadership role. Once you have done so, you have to fill it. Your dog expects it of you.

- a willingness to follow, that is, the tendency to accept one's assigned place within the pack (or human family) and to keep returning to the pack. This faithfulness to the pack is rooted in the instinct to bring things back: Prey is picked up and carried back to the pack. Other canine traits are
- acute, well-functioning senses;
- great alertness;
- good powers of comprehension;
- an impressive memory. In this connection, however, it is important to know that dogs can associate only events that follow each other immediately. Punishment, therefore, must immediately follow a misdeed. Let us not forget one last quality that is crucial for the success of any training program. It is
- the love a dog bears toward its master. Love motivates your dog to become an eager student.

His Master's Voice

Your dog loves to listen to you, especially when you talk to it in friendly tones, which is something you should do frequently. Even though the words have little meaning at first, the dog will listen attentively to your tone of voice and will know instinctively how to respond.

Praise Is the Foundation

During the training session—whether with a puppy or a grown dog—harmony should reign between dog and human. The more relaxed the teacher, the more the dog is ready to learn. Praise is a psychological necessity for every dog; it helps build self-confidence, motivates the dog, and makes it happy. Praise should be the basic attitude and has nothing to do with rewards.

Words of praise and physical praise: While working on an exercise you should praise only verbally. Petting or scratching would distract the dog and interrupt the exercise. When you praise verbally, the words should, as I said before, ring with praise. They have to come from the heart; a dog has an acute telepathic sense and can tell authentic praise from hollow words. Use simple words, and don't feel self-conscious or embarrassed even if a stranger happens to be watching.

A Precise Tone of Voice for Commands

The voice you use for commands should be clearly different from your praising voice. Many commands, like "Come!", "Sit!", and "Stay!" consist of a single syllable and call for a clear, sharp tone. Commands are meant to be obeyed and should sound that way. "Please" has no place in the vocabulary used between human and dog, no matter how polite you may be by nature. I, too, don't always find it easy to omit the "please."

Rebuke Should Be Sharp

Words of punishment or rebuke, like "No!" or "Bad dog!" should be pronounced in a sharp, clipped tone. A dog even learns to distinguish a big "No!" from a little "No!" Use the word "no" only as a reprimand and eliminate it otherwise from your training vocabulary. You can emphasize a rebuke by hitting the ground in front of the dog with your hand or slapping the forbidden object, but never hit the dog. In my efforts to train my dogs, verbal rebuke is the only form of punishment; hitting a dog or shaking it by the scruff of the neck serves only to confuse the animal.

Is Punishment Necessary?

Try to follow me in imagining how a dog thinks.

The situation: A puppy is chewing on a rug. What matters to it is chewing; it has no concept of what a rug is, but chewing is a natural urge. You want to break this habit and are upset about the damage done to your rug. So you scold the dog in a loud voice and smack it.

The dog's reaction: When you started scolding it, the puppy turned its attention to you. The punishment came from you—

the puppy has forgotten all about the rug.

The result: The only thing the puppy will learn if this scene is repeated often enough is that scolding is followed by smacking and that humans can inflict pain. Consequently it will start to respond to your scolding with gestures of conciliation like tail wagging and lowering the head, which anthropomorphizing humans will interpret as signs of a bad conscience or guilt. In fact the dog has neither a good nor a bad conscience, and guilt is an unknown concept to it. None of this has any connection to the rug, which the puppy will go on chewing.

The right way to go about it: The puppy is chewing the rug. You refrain from scolding and, remaining as detached as possible, toss your keys at the dog's rear end. The puppy is startled, and since its entire attention has been focused on the rug it must be the rug that startled it. After a few repetitions of the scene the puppy knows that the rug can cause pain in the rear end. It boils down to this: Whenever you want to break your dog of a bad habit you have to invent a situation that leads the dog to associate unpleasant consequences with the forbidden activity rather than with you. This is easier than you may think. Since lying and underhandedness are foreign to dogs it is easy to trick them as long as you are in control of your movements and facial expressions and keep quiet.

Principles of Punishment

1. What matters is not punishing a dog but making the activity you disapprove of unpleasant enough so that the dog gives it up.
2. Any rebuke has to come at exactly the right moment for the dog to understand what is meant by it.

Opposite page: Training a puppy is as time-consuming as raising a child. In the picture: Heidi with her eight-week-old chow chow puppy.

The Phases of a Puppy's Development

It is impossible to overemphasize—so I repeat it here once more—that the training of dogs is most successful if certain exercises are taught at the right time, for puppies go through stages of development during which they are "imprinted" for the rest of their lives. Making the most of a dog's first year of life for training is crucial, but the first 10 weeks that the puppy spends with its mother and the breeder are equally significant. That is why when you buy a puppy you should check

- if the puppies are living in an environment that resembles what your puppy will find at your house.
- if the puppies are growing up in peaceful, relaxed surroundings.
- if the puppies have plenty of contact with humans. Don't be impressed by a supermodern cage with molded plastic beds for whelping boxes.

Weeks 10–12: Socialization

This is the time when the puppy comes to live with you and when the basic impressions determining the future partnership between human and dog are made. However, contact with other dogs is also important during this period. What do we teach the puppy during these weeks?

- It is housetrained (see page 80).
- It has its first experience walking on the leash (see page 81).
- It gets used to the car (see page 84).
- It should have contact with other dogs (see page 58).
- In frequent games with the puppy we keep taking away the object of play. This teaches the puppy to guard and defend its quarry. To prevent feelings of frustration we make up for the loss of the quarry with praise.

A lot gets crammed into this couple of weeks, but the puppy should not be overworked. Never practice longer than 15 minutes at a time, but never cut a lesson short because the dog has tired of it; always make it finish an exercise that has been started. Consistency and patience are the crucial elements at this stage.

Weeks 13–16: Defining Rank Order

This is the period during which the dog learns most easily that rebuke and punishment follow if it does things that are not allowed. It understands that its master embodies an authority to which it has to subordinate itself and that all praise comes from this person. This period corresponds to kindergarten age in a child's life. If you neglect to assert your authority now, your dog will try to rule the family for the rest of its life.

This is also the time when a dog learns that jumping up on people is not permissible. It learns to obey the commands "Sit!", "Stay!", and "Come!", as well as to stay at home alone and not to beg at the table. In addition you teach it the meaning of "Drop it!" and "No!" (see pages 83–85).

Weeks 17–24: Growing Awareness

This is a critical period during which the puppy becomes aware of the world around it. It becomes conscious of where it is living and reacts nervously and even anxiously to any changes. Don't try to teach it new things during this time but keep reviewing everything that has been learned in the past.

Between the 5th and 6th month (20th to 24th week) a dog begins to develop independence. Preschool is over. The dog is ready for serious learning and needs a firm hand and even more patience than before. Now you can teach it to walk properly on the leash, including turning, stopping, and sitting (see page 83).

Months 6–12: Puberty

During the phase of puberty your dog will act up. It will try to "forget" much of what it learned, rebel, and test whether you are really the boss of the group. If you don't insist on absolute obedience now, you

The most effective way of teaching a dog is through praise. You praise with words or, as in this picture, with gestures.

have botched the training. Starting with the 7th month, male dogs lift their leg to urinate, and bitches may enter their first heat any time now.

In theory your dog should obey all your commands, whether on leash or running free. Let's hope it obeys not only in theory but in practice as well. Now is the time to break the habit of undesired barking. You do this by talking to it soothingly and saying "Quiet, quiet," over and over again.

I have just given you an abbreviated rundown of the best times to teach a puppy certain things. If you have acquired an older dog, there is no reason to despair. Dogs are able and willing to learn into old age, and there is no reason why you cannot, for instance, teach an older dog to walk properly on a leash. Still it is true that the earlier you start training a dog, the easier it will be for you as well as the dog and the better the dog will retain what it has learned.

The basic rules for teaching are:
- Get the dog to understand what it is you want of it.

- Once a dog understands a command, it must execute it.

Note: Never give a command in a pleading voice but always in a firm tone. Yelling is unworthy and unnecessary.

Training a Puppy

Before you can start teaching a puppy the manners it needs to become a pleasant, well-behaved pet, you have to pick it up from the kennel. It is no doubt best if you can pick it up yourself. Don't have it sent to you; puppies are not shipping merchandise (see page 12).

Picking the Puppy Up

Visit the breeder from whom you are buying the puppy at least twice: once to pick out your puppy and then to bring it home. If it is feasible to visit in between to play with the puppy, all the better. At ten weeks the puppy should move in with you. Some ethologists recommend taking the puppy at six weeks, but I think that's too early; many puppies still nurse at that age.

Get the puppy by car, and take along another person to look after it while you drive. Be sure to drive carefully and smoothly. You want the dog to get used to riding in a car and don't want to scare it. It is useful to take a waterproof cover along and to ask for a piece of material or from the kennel so that there is something that smells familiar on the way home. The puppy also needs to be kept warm and comfortable to weather the trip well.

During the first few nights you have to be very firm: the puppy has to get used to its sleeping place. Decide where the puppy is to sleep. If it starts crying and yowling, pet it and try to calm it down, but don't stay too long. After a few nights of disrupted sleep acclimatization will take its natural course. The puppy will soon develop into your dog. Read the chapter on puppy health care (see page 95).

Housetraining a Puppy

Cleanliness and being housebroken are the first things we want to teach a puppy, for puddles on the floor don't make for a happy life together. Being housebroken means that the dog relieves itself only during outdoor walks or in the yard and lets you know if it feels the urge between the normal walk times. It takes about three weeks for a puppy to master this, three weeks during which you must be utterly consistent. Since a full stomach exerts pressure on the bladder, the puppy has to be taken out immediately after every meal. Don't just let the puppy go where it wants but, if possible, carry it to a spot with grass or other soft ground that other-dogs have also selected. If you stick to this habitual spot, the puppy will soon become accustom to it, grasp its purpose, and relieve itself quickly when taken there.

How to carry a puppy: During the first few weeks a mother dog carries her puppies by the scruff of the neck. This method is no longer appropriate by the time we

A puppy's first teacher is its mother. She imparts the basics of good behavior. The picture shows an Airedale terrier with her 11-week-old puppy.

start training a puppy to become house-broken, and it's awkward to boot. Nor should you pick up a puppy under the arms like a baby. The puppy's shoulders are attached to the rib cage only by the serratus magnus muscle. If you pick a puppy up under the arms, you will pull its shoulders away from the body. This hurts. You want the puppy to be comfortable when carried. The best way to go about it is to put one hand under the puppy's rib cage and the other under its rear end.

Don't rush the puppy, and check to make sure it really does urinate or defecate. Don't get upset or discouraged if it refuses to do anything outside and then makes a little puddle or drops some feces as soon as you get back inside.

Be lavish in your praise every time the puppy relieves itself when and where it should. But don't start praising too early, or it may retain some of its bladder's contents to distribute later as it sees fit.

Keep the puppy on the leash when it relieves itself, even if you have a yard where the puppy can go. It will get used to relieving itself this way, which will be useful later on to keep the dog under control. Try using a phrase like "Good job!" when the puppy urinates or defecates. Perhaps it will associate the words with the deed, and it may even learn to do its business on command. This is a convenient word association.

The puppy should be kept warm in its box or basket. A cold puppy has little bladder control. Take it out immediately after it wakes up so that it can make its puddle outside.

During the night the puppy's bed should be close to yours so that you can hear when the puppy wakes up. You'll have to get up too. This is a time of disrupted sleep.

If the puppy relieves itself indoors and you are around, you respond with "No!" But the rebuke has to follow instantly, or it is of no use.

Try to avoid melodramatics. Teaching a dog to become housebroken is not a tragedy; it is hard work. Remove all traces of a "mistake" immediately and scrub the spot with a disinfectant cleanser. The smell of the cleanser will discourage the dog from becoming a repeat offender in that spot. Once the puppy is completely trustworthy, its owners can sigh with relief.

Meeting Collar and Leash

In the course of getting housetrained the puppy has become acquainted with its collar and leash. At first the collar is merely an unpleasant foreign object the puppy would like to eliminate, and the leash is felt as something that limits freedom of movement. At first the puppy on a leash will alternately pull ahead and hang back, trying to dig in its heels. But it has to learn to put up with both collar and leash, for a dog should not be allowed to run free until it reliably obeys commands.

The way to get a puppy used to its leash is to put the collar on the puppy for short periods at first. The best times are when the puppy is playing or eating, because then it is absorbed in pleasant activities. Once it has gotten used to the collar, you can start using the leash.

The first lessons in walking on a leash should take place in a familiar spot either in the house or in the yard. Let the puppy lead you at first; praise it, and keep the leash loose. If anyone is allowed to pull now, it's the dog. The trick is to make the dog think that the restraint it feels is not caused by the leash and the human being on the other end.

Note: Neither the leash nor the collar is a toy. Don't let your dog chew on them because that undermines the authority associated with them.

Training Exercises

Leash

As you can tell by how many dog owners are pulled along by their dogs, pulling on the leash is a privilege of puppydom that many grown dogs are unfortunately unwilling to relinquish. Or, to put it more correctly: It is a habit the owners haven't

"Walking on the leash," done right or wrong? In this picture it's the dog that is taking its mistress on a walk. It hasn't yet been taught the correct way long and persistently enough.

worked hard enough to break. It's not a matter of the dog's learning to heel in the official manner taught in the obedience classes of dog clubs.

What does matter is that the dog learn to respect the radius of the leash, that is, to walk without pulling on the leash. It is also important that the leash not become an "instrument of torture" but be perceived as a vital line of contact with you.

Correction at the right moment helps break the bad habit of pulling. Every time the dog starts leaning into its collar, you pull it back with a forceful yank, but quietly, without shouting. Immediately let the leash go slack again. Pull back again every time the dog surges ahead. This way it will come to associate the sudden jerk, which feels unpleasant, with the collar around its neck, and it will ultimately avoid pulling. I would ask you one thing, though: You should yank forcefully, but do it calmly. The dog is not trying to annoy you by pulling; it simply doesn't know yet what is expected.

If you are too hesitant in correcting this

behavior or if you yank the leash only after the dog has been pulling on it for a while, you will achieve just the opposite of what you want. You are training the dog to have a hard neck that is numbed to pain, and soon you'll have a pulling machine on the leash that will practically yank your arms out of their sockets. I know from experience what hard work that is. Do it right, and break your dog of the habit of pulling.

Walking on Leash

Grasp the handle of the leash with your right hand, pass the leash in front of your body and grasp the leash itself with your left hand, keep the dog on your left side, and start walking (see photograph on page 83). The dog will happily come along. Praise it, but without slowing down your pace. It doesn't much matter whether "the dog's front legs are at a level with the trainer's knees" the way most instruction manuals describe it. After all, you are not out walking with a robot but with a live dog.

Change directions without any command: Simply swivel to the right, and start heading back. Since the leash runs in front of your body from right to left, the momentum of your turn will move the dog around. The dog will immediately catch up with you and follow you attentively. Since all this happens smoothly, the dog will enjoy the maneuver and cooperate happily. Once this is well established, you can proceed.

Stopping and Sitting

When you stop, the dog should sit down. This is particularly important when you have to cross a street. The ideal goal of this exercise is that the dog will sit down without a verbal command when you stop.

This is how you work on it: Hold the leash with both hands in such a way that the dog's head remains slightly raised. Slow down, and then stop. Perhaps the dog will sit down automatically. If not, hold the leash a little more tautly, and gently push down on the dog's rear end with your left hand until the dog sits down. It should sit parallel to you with its head still raised. Then you let the leash go slack slowly and cautiously and say "Good dog siiiit." Wait a second, and then conclude the lesson with praise. The exercise isn't successful until the dog remains sitting.

If the dog doesn't stay seated, terminate the exercise with a "Noooo!" and start it all over. The more strict and exacting you are, the more the exercise will become like a ritual—and dogs love rituals.

Practice the sequence of walking, turning, stopping, and sitting on every walk. Make the dog sit before you cross any street, release it from sitting by saying "Okay" or "Let's go," and then quickly cross the street and stop briefly on the other side, making the dog sit down again. This way the dog learns that the exercise is not over until you reach the other side, and it will remain attentive until then.

Lying Down

A dog that sits down on command will also lie down. The command for this is "Lie down!" or simply "Down!"

Teach lying down by making the dog sit and then pulling its front legs forward with your right hand while pushing its back

This is the way proper walking on the leash looks. The human master determines the speed and the direction, not the dog.

down with your left. Say "Lie down!" and praise the dog when it is lying down. If it wants to get up again immediately, push it down again and say "No!" or "Down!" This exercise can lead right into the next one.

"Stay" (First part)

If you want the dog to continue lying down even when you move away, you command it to "Stay!" Hold your flat hand in front of its face as you say the command. Practice this with constant praise until the lesson has been mastered. Sitting and lying down on command are useful for trips to the veterinarian and especially when the dog is asked up on the examining table. Always make sure that you give the command only when it really will be executed. A command that goes unobeyed or that is not corrected if improperly obeyed can undo much training.

"Stay" (Second part)

The command "Stay" is also used when we want the dog to stay in a room. Practice as described above by holding your flat hand in front of the dog's face and saying "Stay!" Then gradually pull your hand back. If the dog disregards the outstretched hand, you push it back to its place and repeat "Stay!" Go through this routine over and over in all kinds of different situations but always combine the "Stay!" with the signal of the flat hand. The hand signal is a kind of visual command and serves to reinforce the verbal command. The hand signal means the same thing as "Stay!" and should always be executed the same way.

"Go to Your Bed!"

"Go to your bed!" tells the dog to go to its bed and stay there. If the dog goes there of its own free will, you still say "Go to your bed!" and follow the command with praise. If it ignores the command, lead it to its bed, and run through a combination of the "Lie down" and "Stay" exercises.

Vary the tone of the command "Go to your bed!" from soft to emphatic, depending on the situation. As you say it, hold the dog down on its bed with your left hand, first by actually restraining it, later symbolically without touching but just holding your hand over it. Move away slowly while saying "Stay!" and hold your flat hand in front of the dog's face. When the dog has mastered this lesson, you can teach it the visual signal for "Go to your bed!"—namely, pointing with your outstretched arm in the direction of the bed.

"Drop it!" and "No!"

"Drop it!" is used to make the dog drop whatever it has in its mouth—toy, bone, or some unidentified object—whenever you say so and without resistance. Relinquishing booty is against a dog's nature, but in some situations it can be lifesaving. I am thinking about things like sharp bones, plastic, and poisoned bait. The younger the dog when you teach relinquishing, the easier it will be for you to take things from between the growling dog's teeth.

Say "Drop it!" and reach a firm hand across the dog's muzzle, pressing the lips against the teeth and thus forcing the muzzle open. Then praise the dog. Keep repeating this until it has become a smooth routine. This is a lesson that has to become second nature, for if you have to struggle to take booty from a grown dog—especially a member of a big breed—the match will be far more difficult to win than with a puppy. If a dog tries to run away with booty or hide it, you must not let the dog get away with it or let the exercise deteriorate into a game of tag or a mad chase. You have to stay calmly in charge and emerge victorious. If the dog should openly threaten you, punishment has to be swift and clearly come from you.

"No!" is said whenever the dog does something that is not allowed, such as
- urinating or defecating indoors
- picking up garbage
- rolling in dirt
- jumping up on strangers
- barking at the slightest noise
- stealing—not after having stolen, because the "No!" is effective only when the offender is caught in the act.

Use a sharp tone when saying "No!" and reinforce the command by stamping your foot (outdoors) or clapping your hands (indoors). With a particularly obdurate dog "No!" sometimes has to be accompanied by a swat on the head.

Rules for Riding in the Car

A dog has to learn some rules about getting into and out of cars. The rules for getting in are important so that the dog will not let itself be lured into a stranger's car. Getting out properly is important to avoid becoming a traffic hazard.

Keep the dog from jumping into the car by making a visual stop signal—placing your flat hand in front of the dog's face. The dog should respond by sitting down in front of the open car door. When you say "Get in!" it may get in. The dog has to learn not to jump into the car until after the combined commands of "Sit!" and "Get in!"

When leaving the car a reverse order is followed. You open the car door and command "Stay!" The dog is not to leave the car until you say "Come!"

A dog that has been trained to ride in a car (see A Dog in the Car, page 109) regards the car as an extension of its territory and will defend it against strangers the same way it defends your home and property. A dog that is content to stay in the car alone for hours will stay by itself at home, too.

"Come!"

Teaching the command "Come!", which tells the dog to join its master, is easy. Since the puppy wants to be with its master, all we have to do is to go away a few steps and call "Come!" The puppy will catch on quickly. Praise it every time.

These instructions should help you turn your dog into an obedient member of the household. If you are more ambitious, that's fine. Build on this knowledge, and embark on further training.

Formal Training and Dog Trials

Dogs love to learn. You can take advantage of this if you want to train your dog further. Contact dog clubs to find out about the availablility of classes. Join the club of your dog's breed, which will allow you to participate in its training programs and be admitted to its breed shows. How much you do depends entirely on your initiative; your dog is always ready to go.

Dog Shows

If you decide to enter your dog in a dog show, this will give more pleasure to you than to your dog. You get a chance to travel, meet new people, perhaps even win a prize. For the dog, on the other hand, being in a show means nothing but stress. Dog shows are basically opportunities for breeders to display purebred animals, which is important for promoting high quality in breeds. However, it is good if, in addition to professional breeders, who have to enter their dogs in the shows, some dog owners participate "just for fun" so that as many dogs as possible can be seen. To be able to enter a dog in a show the owner first has to join the breeder's club. Through the club you will find out everything you need to know.

In an obedience class, dogs of all breeds, together with their owners, learn how to walk properly on the leash.

Dogs and Their Diet

Not everything that tastes good is good for you. You know that's true for yourself, and, when it comes to food, you can't rely on a dog's instincts any more than you can on your own tastes. Since your dog is living under your care, it is your responsibility to feed it a proper diet.

One has to learn how to feed a dog properly just as one has to learn about a healthy diet for oneself. Neglect of good nutrition is shown by the many obese dogs one sees. Family dogs today are exposed to the same health risks we are. Every third dog is overweight and is eating the wrong foods.

Your dog, whether dachshund, spaniel, or Great Dane, is descended from wolves, and wolves don't live on meat alone. They consume their prey, be it mouse, partridge, or deer, in its entirety, including skin, feathers, and hair, as well as the contents of stomach and intestines and the blood. This supplies them with proteins (from the muscle meat), necessary fats, carbohydrates (from the contents of the intestines), and minerals (from the blood of the killed animal).

Wolves "wolf down" their food quickly and in big chunks, which they regurgitate later in some undisturbed place and eat again at a more relaxed pace. What they cannot eat right away they bury and let cure (a process of chemical breakdown similar to what takes place in the ripening of cheese) to a more easily digestible stage. By watching your dog you will discover traits left over from its wolf past:

- In its anatomical makeup, a dog is still a meat eater, as its teeth and digestive tract show.
- Like a wolf, a dog eats fast, and it often doesn't know when it has had enough.
- A dog easily vomits up excess food it has eaten. This behavior doesn't necessarily indicate sickness.
- Dogs like to bury meat and delight in eating food they dig up again and food that has become moldy. (Meat that has been buried is not toxic, but food rotting in pots is.)
- By eating grass, dogs try to get the same cleansing effect in the digestive tract that they used to achieve by swallowing fur and feathers.

What People Feed Their Dogs

You can't buy prey animals at a store. It is also true that modern family dogs have adjusted more to human food. In spite of this, dogs should eat food that suits their special needs. Although scientists have come a long way in establishing what constitutes a good diet for dogs, dog owners and breeders still fall into four different schools of thinking:

1. Lazy, frugal, or conservative people: They give their dogs leftovers from their own meals, thinking that a dog can live off table scraps. This is the least healthy method of feeding a dog, even if you know somebody whose dog lived to a

Opposite page: A properly fed dog is healthy, strong, and spirited. In the picture: Newfoundland bitch, black and white variety.

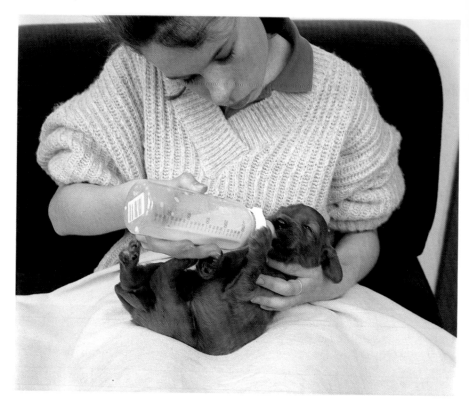

Today bottle feeding puppies (shown is an Irish setter) is no longer problematical, thanks to excellent puppy milk formulas.

very ripe old age under this regimen.

2. Dog owners who regard dogs as pure meat eaters: They give their dogs plenty of muscle and organ meat or bones, which will slowly but surely make the dog sick (constipation, kidney stones, and eczema). Sometimes these owners even feed the meat raw, risking that their pet may get infected with salmonellae or die of Aujeszky's disease (a virus infection that is transmitted in raw pork and, more recently, in beef as well).

3. People who shop and cook especially for their dog: They are convinced that their dog is getting "the best diet possible." Just how good it is depends on how much these owners know about the nutritional needs of dogs.

4. People who rely on commerical dog foods: They take advantage of scientific progress as well as of convenience. This type of diet, which contains all the elements a dog needs in the proper proportions, is first-rate. Gourmets should not compare commercial dog food to our modern fast foods.

Proper Diet for Your Dog

Anybody who eats too much gets fat, and anybody who eats the wrong things gets sick. These laws apply not only to humans, but also to dogs. Concretely, this means: An ideal meal for a dog has to include the basic food groups of proteins, fats, and carbohydrates in the proper proportions. In addition, vitamins and minerals are important. The amount of food given should be just right, so that the dog doesn't get too scrawny or too fat. This all sounds simple and straightforward, but it is not that easy to achieve if you prepare your dog's meals yourself.

There is research today that establishes exactly how many calories dogs of various sizes need. See breed descriptions (pages 128–166).

The ideal dog food, as we know from research studies, should contain at least

30 percent protein, 5 percent fat, up to 5 percent crude fiber (roughage), and at most 50 percent carbohydrates. It should also include 2 percent calcium and phosphorus (as a substitute for the bones of the prey a wild animal would eat). All these substances are present in commercial dog food, which can be given in exactly measured doses (following the instructions on the package). You can, for instance, give a cocker spaniel weighing 26 pounds (12 kg) exactly the right amount of 840 calories it needs.

How Can You Tell If a Dog Is Improperly Fed?

You can tell feeding mistakes by looking at a dog's feces:

- If a dog produces only small quantities of dark, foul-smelling feces, it probably has been getting too much meat.
- Hard, light-colored feces suggest a diet that includes too many bones.
- Large amounts of excreta indicate that the food had little nutritional value.
- Light-colored and runny feces or diarrhea mean: The dog has been drinking milk or has eaten too much liver, lung, raw horse meat, tripe, or udder meat.

Runny stool can be normalized by giving the dog carrot juice or grated apple, mixing bread crumbs into its food, or giving it camomile or weak black tea to drink.

Note: The feces produced by a properly fed dog have a definite shape. They are neither too hard nor too soft, medium brown or lighter, and proportionate in quantity to the size of the breed.

If a dog eats feces, this suggests that it has been getting too much meat. The body reacts to this by overproducing acid, and a natural craving for alkaline substances that will restore the normal balance makes dogs eat carrion or feces, in which acid protein has been converted into alkaline ammonia. Fruits and vegetables also help raise the alkaline level; they should be cooked only briefly.

If a dog is getting obese, people often fail to recognize it in the early stages because the loving eye of the beholder tends not to take in a developing rotundity. There are skinny as well as sturdy individuals in each breed, but a good indicator of normal weight in a dog is its ribs: you should be able to see them or feel them with the tips of your fingers (see also Glossary, OBESE DOGS).

Training a Dog to Develop Proper Eating Habits

To keep your puppy from developing into either a voracious glutton or a picky eater, you have to teach it some "table manners" while it is young. To be sure, inborn factors have something to do with how eager a dog is for food. There are also some breeds that tend to overeat, like spaniels ; and there are some, like setters and small poodles, that are indifferent to food. Castrated males generally tend to overeat.

What is important:

- If you feed your dog consistently at the same time and in the same place, even a born glutton can be kept down to a normal weight. Dogs that routinely get goodies from the table are bound to gain weight and become gluttonous.
- Dogs showing no interest in food can— if the veterinarian concludes that they are not sick—have their appetite stimulated if they are given vitamin B (brewer's yeast in powder form). You can also put something they really like on top of their regular food. Preceding this new regimen with a day of fasting is a good idea.

Some dogs ignore their food until their owner offers them the first few bites by hand. This clearly indicates poor training, but what choice does a loving dog owner have once things have developed this far?

Home-cooked Meals

If you want to prepare your dog's food yourself, you have to cook for the dog every day. Meat, cut into pieces as for stew, is the basis of a proper meal for dogs. Because of the danger of infection, the meat has to be boiled. Beef heart, liver, tripe, and muscle meat are best, but you may occasionally use chicken necks and gizzards as well as fresh-water fish. Add to this cooked rice, whole-wheat bread, or mashed potatoes in the right proportions.

If you are a believer in natural foods and have various kinds of grain in your pantry, you may add oats, barley, or millet to the meat. Use rolled grains soaked for 2 hours in the broth from the meat.

Important additions to the food: One tablespoon sunflower seed oil or lard, brewer's yeast, cottage cheese and bone meal, some blanched vegetables, or some commercial vitamins and minerals.

If you keep varying the composition of the meals, you are right in line with the findings of nutritionists who claim that dogs are not set in their eating habits and enjoy a change. And they, too, like people, develop food preferences and aversions.

Cooking for a dog is not half as difficult as figuring out just how much to serve and what proportions constitute a well-balanced meal. You can look up the number

Young dogs need more nutritious food than fully grown ones, because a great deal of energy is required for physical growth and weight gain. The puppies in the picture are five-week-old German spitz puppies.

of calories in a calorie counter, but finding the composition of some items is almost impossible even with the aid of specialized literature, because some foods like head meat and tripe have never been analyzed in these terms. That is why, over the years, I have become a proponent of commercial dog food, and my dogs have been thriving on it. I don't offer commercial food exclusively; three times a week I give them a meal made up of chicken hearts or gizzards with cereal and vegetable flakes that have been soaked for an hour in the meat broth. My dogs love this special meal, just as they do an occasional serving of tripe. And since dogs have teeth that they like to exercise, I give them occasional small portions of veal ribs with the cartilage left on or a rawhide bone.

Beena the Cocker Spaniel and the Venison Treat

Beena's owner, who had grown up with dogs, swore by home-cooked dog food. In those days dogs were always given raw meat to eat. The authors of her small library on dogs recommended the same, and when she read that the nutritional value of cooked meat was only about two thirds that of raw meat, the matter was settled. She was against commercial dog food. After all, she didn't like food from cans for herself, and she had emotional reasons for her objections as well: Dogs used in laboratories are fed commercial dog food. So she had read somewhere. She took great pains to prepare well-balanced meals, and Beena, though a little on the heavy side and suffering periodically from eczema, seemed healthy enough. Until one day there was an especially delicious dish: raw venison with a few cooked noodles in a cream sauce. Beena came down with a fever, diarrhea and vomiting, and cardiovascular collapse. She was diagnosed as having salmonellosis. After a long talk with the veterinarian—who managed to save Beena's life—Beena's owner now serves her dog only cooked meat and, twice a week, dry dog food.

Note: Meat is no more nutritious raw than cooked. The digestibility of meat

containing connective tissue is even improved by cooking. Raw game presents health hazards, and raw pork and beef can be fatal for dogs (see page 88).

Commerical Dog Food

I have visited a plant of a large dog food manufacturer and was immensely impressed by the general cleanliness of the place, the quality of the basic ingredients, and the checking and scientific precision of the composition of foodstuffs. On every package of commercial dog food the exact composition of the contents has to be listed. My dogs' health and unproblematic digestion are proof to me that I am feeding them right.

What Is Commerical Dog Food?

Commercial dog food is complete; that is, everything a dog needs is contained in it. It is manufactured in three forms:

Canned food (wet), which comes in various flavors.

Semi-moist food, which comes in packets that contain an "average" serving.

Dry food, which can be kept longer and is more concentrated because water has been removed.

In composition, semi-moist and dry dog food is essentially the same as canned.

Since dogs have a much more discriminating sense of smell than we do, experts in laboratories have incorporated into dog food smells that we are unaware of but our dogs respond to.

"My Dog Refuses to Eat Dog Food"

There are in fact some dogs that refuse to eat commercial dog food. The best way to avoid this situation is to give the puppy commercial dog food when it first arrives. One day of fasting can work wonders here. Also, there are many different

brands; the probability is that one of them will appeal to your dog. Once commercial food is accepted, your dog is getting a good diet that is simple to prepare, for

- you save the trouble of cooking.
- you don't have to chop or weigh or calculate anything.
- it takes at most five minutes to serve your dog the best meal money can buy.

Note: That dogs fed on dry dog food are thirstier is not due to saltiness of the food but to the fact that they get less liquid than in other forms of nourishment.

Special Diets for Dogs

Specialists in animal nutrition have developed diets for sick dogs. Your veterinarian may recommend one of the following, depending upon your dog's condition:

- an allergy diet for dogs that can't eat normal dog food;
- a heart diet for dogs suffering from chronic heart ailments;
- a stomach diet to be used for problems of the stomach and intestines and for liver disease;

Two pounds of dog (1 kg): The puppy sitting on the scale is a nine-week-old Yorkshire terrier. It will triple its present weight by the time it is fully grown.

This is what properly nourished puppies look like. From left to right, above: Pekinese mixture, four weeks old; kuvasz, six weeks old. Below: beagle, nine weeks old; wirehaired dachshund, six weeks old.

- a kidney diet for dogs with kidney stones or other urinary problems;
- a convalescent diet for dogs recovering from sickness, for pregnant and lactating dogs, and for puppies before and after vaccination;
- a weight loss diet for obese dogs (see Glossary, OBESE DOGS).

Rules for the Proper Feeding of Dogs

Feeding a dog properly costs money. Depending on the size of the breed and local shopping possibilities you will spend between $1 and $5 a day. Whether you use commercial dog food or homemade meals (regardless of your dog's size) the following rules apply.

1. A grown dog gets one meal a day, if possible at the same time every day.

2. Noon is the best mealtime. This way the dog has plenty of time to relieve itself afterwards and doesn't have to go out in the middle of the night.

3. The food should be neither too hot nor too cold. Room temperature is good. If the dog doesn't finish its food, the next meal should be smaller. A healthy dog is capable of eating half again as much as it really needs.

4. Leftover food should not be left standing. Between meals, the food dish should always be clean and empty.

5. The water dish, however, should always be full of fresh water. A dog has to be able to drink whenever it is thirsty. Dogs should drink only fresh water.

6. Don't give food of souplike consistency. This doesn't contain enough food

value and is not well utilized by the body.

7. A dog needs to rest after a meal. Take it for a walk beforehand; the exercise will stimulate its appetite.

Special Rules for Young Dogs

Between the 10th and 14th week
- a puppy acquires food habits that it will retain for the rest of its life;
- the foundation is formed for strong and healthy bones;
- deficiency diseases arise because of wrong diet;
- a puppy acquires its table manners and learns not to beg.

Young dogs need richer food than adult dogs because quick growth and weight gain require a great deal of energy. That is why high-quality foods are especially important at this stage. Make sure that the the diet includes the necessary vitamins and minerals (especially calcium and phosphorus), as well as proteins in sufficient quantities. All this—in proper dosage and balance—is taken care of if you buy dog food designed especially for puppies. If you start with this food, your dog will get used to commercial dog food at the beginning. You can use commercial puppy food until the dog is one year old.

Feeding Young Dogs

Age in Months	Number of Feedings	First Feeding	Last Feeding
3rd	5	7 A.M.	7 P.M.
4th/5th	2	8 A.M.	6 P.M.
6th/7th	2	9 A.M.	5 P.M.
8th–12th	2	9 A.M.	3 P.M.
over 1year	1 (or 2 smaller feedings)	1 P.M. or 6 P.M.	

The energy and food needs of a puppy during its growth phase are—per unit of body weight—twice those of a grown dog. The following table shows how much your dog should gain per month.

To make proper use of this table you have to weigh your puppy regularly. Small puppies can be placed on a baby scale. For larger, heavier breeds, check your own weight first then step on the scale again with the dog in your arms. The difference between the two readings is the weight of the dog.

Weight Table for Dogs 3 to 9 Months Old

(Average monthly weight gain in pounds (and grams)

Month Breed	3rd	4th	5th	6th	7th	8th	9th
very large	15½ (7000)	13¼ (6000)	13¼ (6000)	11 (5000)	6½ (3000)	6½ (3000)	6½ (3000)
large	7¾ (3500)	7¾ (3500)	6½ (3000)	6 (2750)	5½ (2500)	3¾ (1750)	3½ (1500)
medium	5 (2250)	4½ (2000)	3¼ (1500)	2¼ (1000)	2¼ (1000)	1½ (750)	1½ (750)
small	2¾ (1250)	2¾ (1250)	2¼ (1000)	21 oz. (600)	21 oz. (600)	14 oz. (400)	14 oz. (400)
toy	21oz. (600)	17½ oz. (500)	17½ oz. (500)	8¾ oz. (250)	5¼ oz. (150)	3½ oz. (100)	3½ oz. (100)

If Your Dog Gets Sick

A healthy dog looks and acts normal. In other words:

- It is as active as is typical for the breed.
- It eats with good appetite.
- Its coat is healthy-looking and lustrous.
- Its eyes are bright.

It is your aim and your responsibility to keep your dog healthy. This is done by feeding it properly, taking it for regular walks, taking consistent good care of it, and letting it know that you love it.

How Can You Tell If a Dog Is Sick?

Always observe your dog with a watchful eye, and if you see anything that deviates from the "picture of health," call the veterinarian. It's better to make a few trips too many to the vet's than to neglect going the one time it really counts. A dog can't say "I have a headache" or "My tummy hurts," but veterinarians have learned to diagnose such ailments and to prescribe the best cures possible. You will have to act as interpreter between your pet and the vet. That is why I am giving you some guidelines to help you recognize possible diseases and take appropriate measures at critical moments. For even a dog that is always carefully supervised can get injured, catch a disease, or eat something that will make it sick.

Here are some symptoms that can be signs of various diseases:

Diarrhea can be the result of wrong diet or of eating snow (see also page 42). But it can also indicate an imbalance in the intestinal flora. It takes a veterinarian to diagnose such a case or to determine what is causing blood in the stool (danger of poisoning or coronaviral gastroenteritis!).

Vomiting is not always a sign of illness; it is part of normal canine behavior after eating too much or too fast. Repeated vomiting can be the result of swallowing some foreign object or of poisoning. If vomiting is accompanied by a fever, it is always a symptom of serious disease. Only the veterinarian can determine what the disease is.

Fever always indicates an infection or inflammation, and any animal with a fever should be taken to the veterinarian. Outward signs of a fever are: a coat that has lost its luster; a dry, hot nose; dull eyes; apathy; a noticeable rise in body heat. Take the dog's temperature rectally to get a reliable reading (see page 99).

Dragging the rear end along the ground ("scooting") is usually a sign of constipation or of impacted or irritated anal sacs. Scooting can also be caused by a foreign body, such as a stalk of grass, in the anus, or by a developing abscess (see also page 33). Consult the veterinarian!

Head shaking suggests an accumulation of dried earwax, an ear infection, or a foreign body—a piece of chaff, for instance in the ear. Here, too, the help of a veterinarian is required.

Not shaking after getting up is a bad

Opposite page: Good behavior at the vet's is conduct learned through training. In this picture a Yorkshire terrier is having its eyes examined.

sign for the overall state of a dog's health. Dogs normally shake themselves to get their muscles realigned properly after lying down (see Glossary, SHAKING).

Limping can indicate a sprain, fracture, injury, torn ligament, or a deteriorating joint. Other possible causes include circulatory problems, old age, and hip dysplasia.

Coughing and sneezing are a dog's normal reaction to a foreign body in the throat or nasal cavities or to exhaust fumes. But sneezing and coughing can also be the first signs of a cold or sore throat. If these symptoms are accompanied by a fever, there is a possibility that canine distemper may be the cause (see page 97).

A strong bad odor from the mouth either indicates tooth decay, inflammation of the gums, or a wrong diet; or it may be caused by gastritis. Let the veterinarian take a look at the dog.

A lump can be a harmless pimple or a malignant growth. Since lumps can grow quickly and become dangerous—modern

dogs are prone to cancer—you should consult a veterinarian.

Constant scratching and biting may indicate fleas (see Glossary, DOG FLEAS) or eczema (requiring extended treatment). But since dogs also scratch and bite places that hurt them, it is better to have the veterinarian take a look.

Veterinarian: Your Dog's Family Doctor

If your dog gets sick, it should be treated by an experienced veterinarian. The better the veterinarian knows your dog, the easier it is to recognize a change in the dog's health, diagnose the problem, and initiate proper treatment. That is why you should not change veterinarians once you have found one you trust. You should think of the vet the same way you think of your

Prophylactic health care starts when the dog is still a puppy. The picture shows an apricot-orange toy spitz mother with her puppies.

family doctor. Like most doctors, the vet will not make house calls. Veterinarians prefer to treat animals at their clinics, because dogs are better behaved there than in their home territory.

Just as doctors regard their patients' medical self-diagnoses with skepticism, veterinarians prefer to draw their own conclusions about your pet's ailments. But they do appreciate your telling them exactly what made you decide to call them. Here you have to speak for your dog.

The Visit to the Veterinarian

A well-trained dog allows the veterinarian to do the following without resisting:
- to examine its mouth and ears;
- to lift its paws;
- to lift it up onto a table.

This cooperative behavior is the result of obedience training. There are also some rules you should observe during the visits to the veterinarian:

1. The dog should be clean.

2. It should be kept on the leash in the waiting room.

3. Contact with other animals there should be avoided to prevent danger of infection.

4. Refrain from long-winded descriptions of symptoms and mention only what is to the point.

You will have your first contact with the veterinarian when you take your puppy in to be vaccinated and wormed. That is also the puppy's first meeting with its doctor.

Preventive Health Care: Worming and Vaccinations

Worming

All puppies get roundworms from their mothers. This system devised by nature is ultimately beneficial because it makes puppies develop antibodies to these parasites at the very beginning of life. In nature the problem of worms is automatically regulated, but domesticated dogs have to be taken to the veterinarian. A puppy should be wormed for the first time at eight weeks (if the puppy you are getting is older, ask the breeder if it is already wormed). Four months later the worming has to be repeated. Worms weaken an animal's resistance to infectious diseases. Please check your dog's excrement regularly later on, too, for signs of worms. Roundworms look a little like spaghetti; and segments of tapeworms resemble grains of rice (tapeworms are not as common in dogs as roundworms but should be eradicated at the first sign). Have the dog wormed again if necessary. This is especially important if your dog plays with children.

Vaccinations against Infectious Diseases

Dogs, from the time they are puppies, can catch a number of infectious diseases against which they can and should be protected through regular vaccinations. The five most dangerous of the canine diseases are:

Canine Distemper

This is a virus infection that appears in three different forms:
- as intestinal distemper accompanied by diarrhea;
- as lung distemper accompanied by pneumonia;
- as distemper of the nerves accompanied by paralysis.

Signs: Fever (from 103.5 to 105.°F, 39.7 to 40.8°C), diarrhea, coughing, vomiting, exhaustion, tonsillitis, mucus-laden discharges from the nose, and teary eyes or eyelids that are stuck together. At a more advanced stage, cramps, impaired movements, and disorders ranging from nervous tics to convulsions are observed.

This disease is not limited to puppies. Systematic vaccination programs have made its occurrence much rarer but have not eliminated it.

Different breeds have typical ailments to which they are susceptible. The picture shows a two-year-old French bulldog, a breed that tends to suffer from herniated disks.

Infectious Canine Hepatitis

This disease (also known as H.C.C. for *Hepatitis contagiosa canis*) is also caused by a virus and resembles distemper in its symptoms.

Signs: Fever, inflammations in the oral and nasal cavities, diarrhea, and obvious pain when touched on the abdomen. The vaccine for this disease is always combined with that for distemper.

Leptospirosis

This infection is caused by various strains of bacteria, some of which can spread to humans, causing jaundice.

Signs: Fever; tiredness; vomiting; nasal or ocular discharge; lack of appetite; tonsillitis; stomach, intestinal, and kidney troubles; and often weakness of the hind legs. In severe cases there is also jaundice and impaired movement.

Immunization protects against both getting the disease and transmitting it.

Rabies

This is the most dreaded of all viral diseases, and so far nothing has succeeded in eliminating or containing it.

Signs: Abnormal behavior, unprovoked biting, lethargy, paralysis and cramps, swallowing difficulties. Infected dogs avoid water; therefore one speaks sometimes of "hydrophobia."

Vaccinating dogs against rabies (at four to six months of age, depending upon the state in which you reside) is especially important in order to break the chain of transmission from diseased wild animals to humans. In areas that are declared rabies danger zones, vaccination can save a dog's life, because dogs running loose and suspected of having rabies can be shot. Dogs are allowed to travel abroad only if their vaccination records show that their rabies shots are up to date (see following).

Parvovirus Disease (Canine parvoviral gastroenteritis)

This disease is often transmitted at dog shows and breed screenings where many dogs are gathered (contact with feces, blood or vomit from an infected dog).

Signs: Sudden onset of diarrhea and bloody stool; violent vomiting with the vomit sometimes mixed with blood. The dog becomes apathetic, refuses to eat, and suffers from severe dehydration due to the loss of body fluids.

Since stress contributes to the susceptibility to this disease, dogs from commercial kennels are more likely to come down with it. Parvovirus disease is related to feline distemper. Yearly booster vaccinations are recommended; this protection is usually included in polyvalent vaccines.

A puppy is **properly immunized** if, at eight weeks, and after having been wormed, it receives its first set of shots against distemper, infectious hepatitis, and leptospirosis. This first vaccination should be initiated by the breeder. A second round of the same vaccines should be given between the 12th and 14th week; in areas with rabies danger, a rabies shot has to be included. Booster shots should be given annually against leptospirosis and rabies, and every two years against distemper and hepatitis. The shots don't hurt, and every immunization should be entered in the dog's international vaccination record.

An international vaccination record includes not only information about required immunizations but also the dog's breed and place of birth, as well as the owner's name. This record thus serves both as identification paper and as proof that the dog has been vaccinated against the major infectious dog diseases and—most important—against rabies. This document is issued by the veterinarian, who also enters the kind of vaccines used. All the information is given in English, German, and French.

What a Dog Owner Has to Be Able to Do

There are some medical procedures that the veterinarian can't perform for you and that you have to master in order to take care of your dog. Among these are:

Taking the temperature: The normal body temperature of a dog ranges from 100.8 to 101.8°F (38.2-38.8°C). Anything higher is a fever (see Glossary, BODY TEMPERATURE). Any drop below 100.8°F (37.8°C) is abnormal, and the dog should immediately be taken to the veterinarian.

How to take a dog's temperature: It's easiest to place the animal on a table. Have a helper secure the dog's head with one bent arm and hold the tail up with the other hand. A thermometer lubricated with petroleum jelly is carefully inserted about 3/4 inch (2 cm) into the rectum and kept there for one minute. Try to keep the dog from moving during this time, talking to it and praising it to reassure it.

Giving medication in the form of powders and pills: Wrap some cooked hamburger meat around the medicine and place the ball of meat as far down the dog's throat as possible. Make sure the dog actually swallows it.

Pills can be given with or without the meat wrapping. If you give pills straight, open the dog's mouth, pull back the upper lip, and push the lower jaw down; then place the pill as far back on the tongue as you can. Then close the dog's mouth and gently hold it shut. A friendly pat at that same moment distracts the dog and makes it swallow. But watch out; some dogs spit out a pill as much as a full minute after it has been given.

Here is another method: Take a piece of cooked meat, cut a slit into it, and stick the pill in the slit. Then give it to the dog.

Giving drops or other liquids: Place drops on the tip of the dog's tongue or farther back behind the canine teeth.

When giving **liquids,** pull the lower lip of one side out a little to make a small pocket, then slowly dribble in the medicine. Keep the dog's head slightly raised as you do this.

Giving suppositories: Again a helper is useful. While one person tries to keep the dog calm, petting it or holding it on the lap, the other pushes the suppository with one finger slowly as far as possible into the rectum. Wear a disposable rubber glove

A bandage has to be put on properly and stay in place. The vet can do this best.

for this. You may want to push it in a little further with a rectal thermometer. Then hold the tail against the anus so that the dog won't push out the suppository.

Reassuring contact and physical restraint during examinations or treatments: Keep talking to the dog constantly during the procedure and keep a reassuring and firm hand on its neck. If the dog is to be held as still as possible, you can take it into your arms so that its head is encircled by your arm and faces away from the person treating it. Hold on to the dog's shoulder with your other hand. Dogs that might panic or bite should wear restraining muzzles. If the dog is supposed to lie down to be treated, place it on its side, stand at its back with your forearms on top of its side, and, with your hands, hold onto the two legs that are flat against the table. This way you can keep even large dogs down without exerting great force. But it is very important to maintain a calm and reassuring mood.

How to bandage a dog's muzzle: Use a strong bandage or necktie about 3 feet (1 m) long. Lay it over the dog's muzzle, tie a simple knot under the chin, cross the ends, and tie them behind the ears.

How to put on a pressure bandage: Place a sterile gauze pad directly on the wound and wrap the bandage several times over it. Place some additional absorbent cotton over the wound every third time you run the bandage across it. Twisting the bandage material every so often ensures good, tight pressure. (Amateurs usually leave bandages too loose.) If the wound continues to bleed in spite of the bandage, the blood supply has to be cut off between the wound and the body (use a tourniquet, suspender, or a similar elastic but firm material). The bandage has to be loosened briefly every 30 minutes.

Any dog that has been injured in an accident should immediately be taken to the veterinarian!

The Trip to the Veterinarian

Dogs are not fond of visits to the vet even if they have had no bad experiences there. Other nervous dogs there and the smell of fear and medications inspire anxiety even in otherwise fearless dogs. That's why any dog should always be kept on a secure leash.

For transporting an injured dog you can use a large, open cardboard box. Line it with a blanket. A bag with handles or a basket will do for carrying a small dog.

Take the dog in a car, and take along another person if any procedure is required. This person can hold and comfort the dog on the way home.

Large cities often have **pet taxis, animal transportation services, or veterinary ambulances** (telephone numbers available from local animal protection organizations) that will take animals to the veterinarian for owners who don't drive. A veterinary ambulance can also be of great help in accidents. If there is no such ambulance, an injured or unconscious dog has to be placed on its side on a blanket and is then carried by two persons with great care, as on a stretcher. Please move as cautiously as you can when transporting a dog like this, avoiding jolts to spare the animal pain. If a dog is unconscious, you have to pull its tongue out of its mouth so that it won't choke to death on it.

Spaying or Injections to Eliminate Estrus?

To prevent your female dog from having unwanted puppies you can do one of the following:

The veterinarian can administer hormone treatments that suppress ovulation. Injections are given every four to five months, depending on the kind of dog and the length of its sexual cycle. Your veterinarian can furnish you with more detailed information.

Sterilization, a surgical procedure in which the fallopian tubes are tied off. This prevents fertilization of the eggs but does not eliminate estrus and can in fact result

in permanent estrus.

Spaying, that is, removal of the ovaries, is the procedure that is now being recommended by most veterinarians. It is *the* answer if a dog has had several false pregnancies or if there is suspicion of unwanted pregnancy. This operation is as routine these days as removing an appendix and is recommended even before onset of the first breeding cycle (see Glossary, ESTRUS). The psyche of the dog is completely unaffected, and diseases of the uterus brought on by age are eliminated. Since there is no such thing as menopause in canines, bitches that are not spayed go into heat and can have puppies even when very old.

Abnormal Behavior

Psychological disorders are not the exclusive prerogative of humans. Our hectic life-style, stress, and many other negative aspects of modern life are taking their toll on dogs, too, and can lead to disturbed behavior. Here are telltale signs of mental disorders:

- excessive aggressiveness
- destructiveness in the apartment
- excessive timidity
- excessive watchfulness and constant barking
- running off and roaming
- chasing bicycles and cars
- compulsive eating
- fear of other dogs and other deviations from normal dog nature.

Tracing the origins of abnormal behavior is as difficult as successful treatment, for mental disorders are seldom inborn. Sometimes breeders are at fault if they raise excessively sensitive or aggressive animals. But more often than not we ourselves are to blame for flaws in our dogs. Here is a list of human mistakes that can harm a dog psychologically and that you should avoid:

Keeping a large dog in a small apart-

Breeds of unusual appearance have their distinctive problems. In a Shar-Pei (depicted here), for instance, you have to watch out for eczema in the skin folds.

ment: This leads to a buildup of aggressive energies if you don't work or exercise with the dog at least two hours a day.

Mood changes: If you are ill-humored or subject to radical changes in mood, your dog won't know what to expect of you. It doesn't "understand" you and reacts in confused and unnatural ways.

Frequent weekend excursions to new and different places may be exciting at first but will eventually be wearing for your dog.

Walks that keep getting shorter mean a reduction of the dog's territory to which the dog responds with resentful incomprehension.

Irregular habits: Dogs need to have dependable routines in their lives, like walks and mealtimes at the same time every day. Changing the schedule continually is upsetting to the dog's mental balance.

Changes in the family caused by marital conflict, temporary separation, and divorce can make a dog sick (as it does people).

Chinese hairless dogs compensate for their lack of fur by having a higher body temperature. They are more robust than they look.

Lack of authority and lax training lead to an aggressive and arrogant attitude in the dog.

Extreme pampering by one person: The dog develops a jealous possessiveness and reacts to other people aggressively.

Please stop here for a moment of soul-searching. Are there any other weak spots in your life with your dog? Always treat your pet justly, consistently, and never thoughtlessly. This is the best way to maintain its mental health.

The Dachshund that Bit Its Owners

A recently married couple purchased a dachshund. Soon the dog began to defend its food by growling, which its masters found cute. Then one day the dog started to bite them when they tried to take the food dish away. This not-letting-anyone-take-the-food is natural dog behavior. The mistake the dachshund's masters made was that they didn't immediately and clearly establish who was at the top of the family hierarchy. In a wolf pack a higher-ranking animal may take the food of a lower-ranking one. This rule is established by the stronger animal's repeatedly taking food and punishing resistance until this behavior is taken for granted. The dachshund, which was not punished and which developed considerable self-importance, took to selecting its own sleeping place: First it was under, then on top of its mistress' bed. Now the husband, if he as much as approached the dog's sleeping place, got bitten. Later the dog started biting when it was not taken along on a walk. The couple was desperate. They made an appointment at a veterinary clinic, where it was explained to them how they could break the dachshund's claim to hierarchical superiority through proper punishment. The couple succeeded within two weeks. There was one final rebellion, which was quelled. Since then the dachshund and its family have been living together happily.

Note: How do you think the story would have ended if the dog were a Great Dane, a rottweiler, or a German shepherd?

Dogs and Hygiene

I have already touched on this subject in connection with "A Dog and a Baby" (see page 15), where it is of most importance. In general, hygiene is nothing to get hysterical about. On the other hand, you should not forget about it completely. Neither human beings nor dogs are sterile creatures. People and their dogs live in the same microbiological environment and develop mutual immunities. Studies have found, after careful parasitological and microbiological examinations, that hygiene tends to improve rather than deteriorate in a household when a dog joins the family. At this point people always ask me: What about the diseases that are transmitted by dogs?

Zoonosis is the term applied to infectious diseases that can be transmitted back and forth between people and animals. If such a disease is found in a dog, the veterinarian treats it; the same disease in humans is treated by a physician. The best protection against these diseases is

- observing basic rules of cleanliness when handling a dog: wash your hands regularly, and don't let the dog lick your face;
- regular immunization of the dog;
- careful worming;
- feeding the dog only cooked meat.

Roundworms from puppies that have not been wormed can pass on to small children if physical contact is too close and if the children happen to swallow worm eggs.

The eggs of canine tapeworms are transmitted to dogs through raw meat or mice the dogs eat. Tapeworms are transmitted to humans through ingestion of meat, too. Eating raw meat represents a greater danger of infection than dogs that carry the parasite.

Ringworm (dermatophytes) can be passed back and forth between dogs and humans. They show up as ring-shaped, red patches that itch. Treatment is rather long and difficult.

According to the most recent research, dogs have very little to do with the transmission to humans of **toxoplasmosis,** an infectious disease caused by a protozoan parasite. Instead, the disease is spread through uncooked pork and through the excreta of cats. Since it is possible for toxoplasmosis to be transmitted congenitally to the human fetus by infected mothers, gynecologists have developed tests for this disease that you can ask to have done.

Since **tuberculosis** has been largely eliminated in humans, dogs no longer get infected by people and are therefore no longer a source of infection for humans.

Rabies and one specific form of leptospirosis (*Leptospira icterohaemorrhagiae*) are two of the five major canine diseases against which you have to vaccinate your dog regularly (see page 98) and which can be transmitted to humans. Immunization of the dog then protects humans against contracting either dis-

An eight-week-old Old English sheepdog with one brown and one blue eye. Supposedly, blue eyes are immune to cataracts.

The life cycle of a boxer: On the left, a young male at eight months; at right, a fully grown boxer at five years of age.

eases from the immunized dog.

Tonsillitis and mumps can, just like colds and the flu, spread from humans to dogs and vice versa. Dogs are more at risk here than humans.

About Getting Old and Dying

One of the most frequent questions relating to dogs and dog breeds is: How long do dogs live? It's a question I can't really understand. After all, I don't ask people how long they expect to live. The answer to the question about the life expectancy of dogs is actually quite depressing. The average dog lives only seven years. (This average statistic takes into account diseases of infancy, accidents, and so on.) The Methuselah among dogs is the Tibetan terrier (Lhasa Apso), which can live up to 20 years. A good average age is 10 to 14 years. Giant dogs and bulldogs live only seven to nine years (again a statistical average).

How much is a year in the life of a dog?

Nine years of a dog's life are the equivalent of 58 human years. The old rule that one dog year equals seven human years is still often quoted but it is not accurate. After 12 months a dog is essentially fully grown, and after that one dog year equals

five human years.

Dogs begin to turn gray when they are about six. The gray first appears around the lips and on the chin; then it spreads across the cheeks and nose and reaches the area around the eyes by the time a dog is eight to ten years old. The forehead and the rest of the head turn gray in dogs older than that. Working dogs turn gray earlier than companion dogs.

When a Dog Gets Old

A dog is considered old when it is about 12. Since dogs perceive the world mostly through their noses and the olfactory sense is usually not affected by age, fading eyesight and diminished hearing bother the animal less than they would a person. But the bones and joints are not as strong as they used to be, and the dog is slowing down on walks. Sometimes a dog's housetraining is also not as reliable as in earlier years. In an old dog, this has nothing to do with training; it is simply a weakness of the physical system. On the other hand, an old dog is focused almost entirely on us and has come to resemble us more and more. It knows everything, understands everything, and sometimes is as playful as in earlier days. This is the reason why it is so hard to take leave of an old, familiar pet, whether death claims it directly or whether we have to step in to cut short needless suffering.

Putting a dog to sleep by giving it a dose of anesthetic appropriate to its size and weight is today such a well perfected procedure that the animal is not aware of anything unusual, and a loving owner can hold the dog until the breathing has stopped. We owe it to our pets to stay with them to the end.

How Our David Died

On Saturday he was catheterized once more, but our vet gave us little hope. David was very quiet and spent much of his time in our large garden, where he lay either under some bushes or hidden in the tall grass. Monday night my wife went to bed on a mattress on the floor of the sick chamber we had set up downstairs; David joined her and slept through the entire night quietly, cuddling close to her like a puppy. He had stopped wagging his tail two days before and wagged it only once more ten minutes before he died, when a male mongrel puppy came up to him in the waiting room at the vet's. We held him in our arms. Then the vet gave him the shot. He went to sleep quickly and quietly. His last breath was as deep as when he used to go to sleep fully contented. He lay on his side and looked as though he were sleeping soundly. Only he wasn't breathing anymore. And his face had suddenly aged. Everything else about him was soft, and his paws were bent in embryo position. In the car on the way home I sat in the back seat with him, just as during every other trip home from the vet's. My gestures of comfort no longer reached him. I wrapped him in the brown blanket on which he had slept all the years he was with us and which he had defended first against Henry and later against Stasi. I felt almost closer to him than ever before as we took leave of him. When I carried him to his grave, rigor mortis had just set in.

When I saw the grave Alfred had dug next to Henry's, I could see through my tears how large a dog he had been, our little one.

Double spread on following page: Two imposing looking dogs: a cream-colored and a red chow chow.

A venerable male boxer 12 years of age. He is almost blind, quite gray, and suffers from arthritis.

Traveling with a Dog

Going on Vacation with Your Dog

Unless you find a really good place to leave your dog or have relatives or friends willing to move into your apartment for the time you are gone, you cannot leave your dog behind. A dog simply doesn't understand what is going on if you take off for a couple of weeks. Those two weeks are an eternity for the dog. On the other hand I would not, of course, recommend that you take your dog along on a trip to the tropics or on a rugged expedition.

If for absolutely imperative reasons—I know you would not do this lightly—you have to board your dog at a kennel, ask the advice of friends who have had experience in this line. Good boarding kennels are rare. Consult your veterinarian, or write to the American Boarding Kennel Association (ABKA). A list of approved kennels in your area can be obtained by writing the ABKA at 4575 Galley Road, Suite 400A, Colorado Springs, Colorado 80915.

Preparing for the Trip

You need an international vaccination record (see page 99) for any trip that involves crossing the border to another country. Since regulations governing the entry of animals into various countries change frequently, it is best to inquire at the consulate of the country in question.

As a responsible dog owner, you will find that most of the required vaccinations will already have been taken care of.

Some countries also require a statement from a public-health veterinarian that the dog is healthy.

You cannot vacation with your dog in England, Norway, and Sweden. These countries demand a quarantine period of at least four months.

If you plan to stay with your dog in a hotel or inn or on camping grounds, you should phone or write ahead of time to ask if pets are welcome and ask for a written permission to be sent along with your reservation papers. For more information consult the Dictionary of Hotels that Accommodate Guests with Dogs, "Touring with Towser," available from Gaines TWT, P.O. Box 8172, Kankakee, Illinois 60901 (Price $1.50).

The Dog's Luggage

You will have to pack not just for yourself but for the dog as well. The following should be included whenever you are traveling with your pet.

- the dog's food and water dishes because the dog is used to them;
- its blanket and one or two towels for its exclusive use;
- a bottle of water for the trip;
- a first-aid kit with drugs against motion sickness and diarrhea. Also take along an antiseptic powder, eye drops, and flea spray or powder;
- an address tag with the home and vacation addresses to be attached to the collar.

On the Train or Airplane

Before a train trip you should inquire how your dog may travel, for there are different rules for large and small dogs. You can take your small dog along without any problems in a traveling container; larger ones must travel in a container in the baggage car. Find out what regulations apply and whether or not you may visit your dog en route.

In airplanes. Here again, you should check the various arrangements before you purchase tickets. The national ASPCA and your local travel office has a booklet that provides advice about appropriate container sizes. Some airlines lend containers; others rent them. Larger dogs are transported in the baggage compartment. Whether you want to subject your dog to this way of traveling is up to you. I wouldn't do it. Be sure, in any case, to find out well ahead of time from the airline or the travel office what regulations are *currently* in effect.

At the Vacation Resort with Your Dog

Dogs, like people, take some time to adjust to a geographically different environment. Remember, if you come from the north, that your dog is not used to southern heat, and don't impose physical exertion on it during the middle of the day. Inquire if there are local dogs that are running loose. And take other vacationers into consideration: If dogs are allowed on the beach, make sure your dog doesn't bother other bathers.

A Dog in the Car

In the life of a modern companion dog the car plays an important role. There are many safety and comfort considerations.

Extensive Vacation Trips

No matter how many miles you have set yourself to cover in a day, the dog that is traveling with you has to be able to relieve itself and wander around a bit four times a day. These rest stops are equally important for people. A rule that must never be broken is that dogs always get in and out of cars on the curb side. Another rule is that the dog gets into the car first, then the baggage and the passengers. When leaving the car, the order is reversed: first the people, then the dog.

On short walks taken during the trip you should always keep the dog on a leash. Letting the dog run free can lead to an accident. Besides, the dog is on unfamiliar territory, and if it comes across an exciting track and runs off, it may be lost for good. Even if the consequences are not that dire, you can still lose a lot of time looking for the dog.

If you stop at a parking lot or a rest stop along the highway, take your dog a long enough distance away so that what it eliminates will not be a nuisance to other travelers. The same applies to stops near roadside restaurants. Inside these restaurants, the same rules should be followed as in other eating establishments. You may take your dog inside only if

- dogs in general are permitted.
- your dog is well enough trained not to bother others and remains as inconspicuous and quiet under your seat or table as possible.
- if it enters on a leash and stays on the leash.
- if you don't let it eat off dishes meant for guests. A waitress in a place that allows dogs will bring you a bowl with water or fill the one you bring along.

If your car breaks down, make sure your dog cannot wander away from the car. Either leave the dog in the locked vehicle or have somebody riding with you take the dog for a short walk. If both you and your passenger(s) are needed to fix the car, tie the dog to a tree or bench or whatever is handy. Tie it far enough away that it won't get in the way of your repair efforts or, in well-meant zeal, attempt to protect the car against strangers who are trying to help you. And don't forget the tied dog when the car is fixed and you are ready to take off again.

If you travel on a ferry you have to observe the regulations in force there. On long rides you can usually keep the dog with you either on deck (always on a leash) or in your cabin. For shorter trips the dog stays in the car. Dogs, like small children, are immune to seasickness.

If your dog starts getting restless on a long journey on high-speed highways, it may be for one of the following reasons:

- Traveling so fast can have awakened its passion for hunting. That is one explanation experts in animal behavior have put forward.
- The constant whirr produced by tires revolving at high speeds—which humans don't hear—may be bothering your dog. By changing the traveling speed, the sound frequency of the whirr can be modified, which may help calm your dog down.
- Self-assertive dogs are restless because the moving car forces motion upon them while they themselves have to remain inactive. A stop with a brief walk and some obedience exercises

The car should become a dog's second territory. If a dog is transported in a station wagon—like the Hovawart in this picture—it needs a pad or other surface on which it does not slide around.

("Sit!", "Lie down!") restores discipline. It is also helpful if the dog has a place in the car where it cannot look out while the car is moving.

- The style of driving (sudden braking, accelerating unevenly, going around curves too fast) also affects the well-being of your dog during the trip.

The Best Place in the Car

The best and safest spot for a dog is on the floor of the front seat on the passenger's side, if possible on the dog's blanket. Here there are no drafts and there is the least shaking. If you have to slam on the brakes, the dog doesn't go flying through the air but is stopped by the wall. Also, the close presence of the dog's owner has a reassuring effect, and the legs of the person in the passenger seat provide body contact with a human. The dog in this position cannot be so large, of course, that there is no room left for the person's legs.

A large dog belongs in the back of the car, where—if the car has front-wheel drive and there is no drive-shaft tunnel—

the dog should stay on the floor. In a station wagon, the dog can lie in the back section. But it has to lie on something that it can get a grip on. If neither of these possibilities works, the dog should sit or lie on the back seat on its blanket, which you have to tuck in the crack between the seat and the back rest well enough so that it won't slide. If the dog has a tendency to climb around in the car, you should put a leash on it that is short enough to keep it from jumping off the seat and strangling itself on the leash. There are also special grates and nets to be used with restless dogs to keep them from climbing into the front seat and bothering the driver. If you train your dog as a puppy to sit in a certain place, it will regard this place as its own and become a good passenger.

Where a dog should never sit (I have not made up these examples):
- in the driver's lap;
- between the driver and the door with the head sticking out the window;
- in the front passenger seat;
- on the shelf underneath the back window. In a collision even a dachshund riding there could become a deadly missile for everyone in the car;
- the trunk of a regular car. A dog can't see anything there and gets too little air.

A Car That Is Safe for a Dog

The more window area a car has, the hotter it gets in the summer. If you don't have air conditioning, you have to leave the windows open, and if there is a dog riding in the car, this is not without dangers. Dogs like to stick their heads out and easily get conjunctivitis from the fast-moving air. A dog obviously becomes a general traffic hazard if it suddenly jumps out of an open car window. Dogs have been known to jump out of moving vehicles because they caught sight of another dog.

Ventilation screens made of sturdy plastic can prevent such accidents. Folded up, they are small enough to fit in the glove compartment. They are clamped in the half-open window and provide fresh air even in a parked car.

They also serve to prevent anyone from reaching into the car.

Seat belts for dogs: Today there are even seat belts for dogs that offer greater safety to both the dog and the people in the car in case of an accident. An accident involving a car traveling at 31 m.p.h. (50 km.p.h.) would probably be fatal to an unrestrained dog, whereas a dog wearing a seat belt would probably get away with only a few broken bones or bruises.

Seat belts, available in the better pet stores, consist of a belt attached to the back of the seat, a restraining belt, and a harness across the chest. They can be installed in any car and are easy to use. They come in several sizes and can accommodate anything from a Yorkshire terrier to a Saint Bernard. The dogs still have some freedom of movement when belted in, so that they can either sit up or lie down.

A net between the front and back seats keeps your dog from moving up front with you. These elastic nets stretched over a metal tube frame are designed for specific car models and are available for almost any station wagon or for hatch-backs with large enough slanted hatch openings. For other types of cars there are universally usable nets with elastic ropes around the edges. The nets are attached to four hooks and can be used in two-door models and sports cars.

Grates of metal bars, either permanently installed or clamped into place by bars whose length is adjustable can be used to create a "dog compartment" in the car. (Safety depends on how solidly the grate is installed.) Grates of this kind are now available for just about any type of car.

Tub-shaped safety blankets for the car prevent your dog from
- climbing into the front of the car
- sliding between the front and back seat if you have to brake suddenly
- dirtying the car upholstery

Using seat belts, nets, grates, or safety blankets in a car is important for the life and safety of your dog, because you never know when an accident might happen.

Glossary

This is an alphabetical list of entries followed by brief explanations that will expand your knowledge about dogs and your ability to take proper care of your dog.

A

Aggression
This term describes the instinct to attack and fight. According to Konrad Lorenz it is "an instinct like any other and, under natural conditions, just as important to the survival of the individual and the species." In some breeds, as in hunting dogs (including dachshunds) and guard dogs, it is a desirable quality that has to be channeled in the right directions through training. The negative side of aggression is that it can become so exaggerated that dogs endanger the world around them. Aggression can also degenerate into psychological disorders (neuroses) as in fear biters, which actually bite rather than just threatening to bite, especially if they are tied or restrained on a leash. See BITING.

Ailments associated with certain breeds
Ailments that occur with greater frequency in some breeds (see Breed section, pages 128–166).

AKC
American Kennel Club. This organization serves as an umbrella for all of the breed clubs in the United States.

Alpha animals
This is a term used by ethologists to describe the top-ranking individuals (both males and females) in a pack of animals. "Alpha" is the first letter of the Greek alphabet. The term is also applied to very assertive dogs.

American-bred Class (official show class)
Open to dogs that are not champions, six months of age or over, whelped in the United States after a mating that took place in the United States.

Anal face
The area under the tail, which serves as a kind of identification card for a dog. It is the most important place to sniff during social encounters, which always involve an anal check. Sniffing another dog's anal area is the prerogative of high-ranking male dogs (see Rules Dominating Dog Encounters, page 59).

Anal Glands
Various glands near the anus producing scent substances that permeate the feces and arouse the dogs' interest in each other's feces and anal region. If the glands are overly full or clogged, the dog drags its rear end along the ground (see page 33).

Animal shelter
Shelters set up by organizations to prevent cruelty to animals, where homeless animals can stay and are fed temporarily until new owners are found.

Apron
The longer hair which forms a frill at the base of the neck in certain breeds, i.e., rough collies.

B

Bat ears
Longish, erect ears, broad at the base and

with rounded tips (resembling those of a bat). French bulldogs have bat ears.

Biting
Estimates by pediatricians about how many children are accidentally bitten by dogs are surprisingly high. School-age children run the greatest risk. Injuries are seldom serious, and the offender is usually the family's dog or a neighbor's dog. The reason for the accidents is insufficient acquaintance with canine behavior.

In addition, every year thousands of mail carriers are bitten by dogs. Small dogs, like dachshunds, poodles, or small mongrels are especially aggressive. Scientists don't yet have an explanation for this. One reason dogs are so suspicious of mail carriers may be that they accumulate so many different scents on their rounds from house to house. Another guess is that mail carriers come and leave without talking to anyone and that dogs think of them as thieves.

Blaze
Thin white stripe on the forehead, typically dividing the eyes.

Bloodline
Refers to a line of purebred ancestors as recorded in the registration papers. The term was coined when it was still incorrectly assumed that the blood was the carrier of genetic traits.

Bloom
Gloss on the coat of healthy dogs.

Blue merle
Blue and gray marbled with black. Found in collies, Great Danes, and dachshunds (tiger dachshund). The gene responsible for the merle factor is often linked to genetic defects, such as blindness and deafness.

Body language
A dog's various postures as interpreted by ethologists constitute canine body language (see INTIMIDATION DISPLAY and INVITATION TO PLAY).

Body temperature
The normal body temperature of adult dogs lies between 100.8 and 101.8°F

(38.2–38.8°C). Anything above 103°F (39.5°C) is a fever and requires the attention of a veterinarian unless it is clearly a result of momentary excitement (female dogs). If the temperature of a sick dog drops below 100°F (37.8°C), this is abnormal and a bad sign (see also Taking the temperature, page 99).

Bond to humans
The attachment a puppy forms to people originates very early, between the third and the seventh week of life. During this time a puppy should have contact with some humans. Dogs adjust to humans between the eighth and twelfth week. This is why you should not delay picking up and holding your puppy (see page 78).

Bones
The symbol of what dogs supposedly like to eat. In fact, bones have been shown to be a less than ideal form of dog food because they interfere with the proper functioning of the digestive system, as the white feces of dogs that have eaten too many bones show. The argument that dogs should be given bones to exercise their chewing muscles on something natural no longer carries much weight now that there are rawhide bones, which are digestible. Soft veal bones are a natural alternative.

Bred-by-Exhibitor Class (official show class)
Open to all dogs, except champions, six months of age or over that are exhibited by the same person, or immediate family, or kennel that was the recognized breeder on the records of the American Kennel Club.

Breed
A subgroup of a species of domestic animals that differs from other subgroups by having certain distinguishing traits. Subjective criteria determine how individual breeds are defined.

Breed Clubs
National canine clubs, each of which is dedicated to a particular breed. Under the auspices of a national umbrella organization (such as the American Kennel Club in

the USA), it sets the standards for the respective breed.

Breed defects
Breed defects occur when selective breeding to achieve some "ideal of beauty" or an "original look" results in physical weaknesses or defects. Some examples of this are: French bulldogs, which have large heads and narrow pelvises, which means their puppies have to be delivered by Caesarean section; Boston terriers, which are also afflicted with birth complications and often get keratitis (inflammation of the cornea) because of their protruding eyes; brindled Great Danes, dachshunds, and collies, which are often deaf and blind (see BLUE MERLE. Chow chows and Shar-Peis have pathologically narrow eye slits; basset hounds as well as Saint Bernards tend to have a gaping space between the eyeball and the lower lid; and German shepherd dogs are subject to HIP DYPLASIA. Reasonable breeders manage to avoid such defects without changing the appearance of their dogs to any significant degree from the breed ideal.

Breeder
The owner of a purebred bitch at the time she is bred or gives birth to a litter.

Breed screening
A thorough examination of a young dog, especially of a working breed, to see if a dog can be used for registered breeding.

Breed standard
See STANDARD.

Brindle
Stripes formed by darker hair in a lighter coat, such as black and brown, as in Great Danes, bulldogs, boxers, and bullterriers.

Brisket
Underpart of the chest (beneath forelegs).

Broken
The irregular patterning of the coat.

Brush
Thick tail, resembling that of a fox.

Burr
Inner part of the ear.

Butterfly nose
Blackish nose, with pinkish areas.

Button ears
Medium-long ears, set high on the head, with the ear flap folding forward. Pugs have button ears.

C

CAC
Stands for Certificat d'Aptitude au Championat, awarded to dogs that are eligible to participate in national competitions for appearance.

CACIB
Stands for Certificat d'Aptitude au Championat International de Beauté, awarded to dogs that are eligible to participate in international competitions for appearance. This is the most important competition at international shows.

CACIT
Stands for Certificat d'Aptitude au Championat International de Travail. This is a rarely awarded certificate of eligibility for the international championship for working dogs.

Calluses
Larger dogs develop calluses on their elbows and hocks if they sleep on a hard bed. These calluses can get infected. Give the dog a softer bed and have infections treated by a veterinarian.

Calorie requirements
A 22-pound dog (10 kg) needs about 740 calories a day. When out walking, a dog uses up six calories per .6 miles (1 km). Running takes three times as much. (See Dogs and Their Diet, page 87).

Canine teeth
Long and sharp teeth situated at the corners of both jaws.

Carrion
Eating carrion is an annoying habit that dates back to the dogs' feral past, when carrion served to restore the system's acid/alkaline balance. The low-protein substances in carrion and manure relieve acidity in the organism that has developed as a result of a one-sided diet (see page

89). Unlike spoiled meat, carrion (meat that has ripened) is not poisonous.

Carrying
Small dogs can be carried on one's arm with the dog's rear end resting on the lower arm while the hand supports the dog's chest. For visits to the veterinarian or for longer distances a carrying bag is better.

Larger dogs are carried by putting one hand between the dog's hind legs and supporting the belly, while the other grasps the dog's rib cage between the front legs.

Injured or unconscious dogs are placed on their side on a stretcher, covered with a blanket, and carried by two persons.

Cataract
A clouding of the eye's lens, usually brought on by old age.

Cat-foot
A small, compact foot that is rounded like a cat's. Typical of border terriers, chow chows, Dalmatians, pugs, the spitz group, and whippets.

Champion
Winning title awarded to dogs that most closely resemble the STANDARD of their breed.

Character
Sum of the qualities and peculiarities that dogs of a particular breed typically exhibit. Character includes temperament, eagerness to learn, persistence, and combativeness or exceptional affection. It is the character that determines whether or not a breed is suitable for a certain person (see Breeds, page 128–166).

China eye
A clear blue eye.

Choke collar
Consists of a chain loop that tightens when the dog starts pulling on the leash. Collars with spurs on the inside are used for training particularly obstinate dogs and should be used only with great caution.

Color strains
Different coat colors found in the same breed, as in cocker spaniels, greyhounds, and poodles.

Constitution
Inherited physical qualities, resistance to external influences, physical stamina. A dog's constitution belongs to the individual dog rather than to the breed and is unchangeable.

Copulation
Copulation between dogs can last from 10 to 45 minutes. The swollen penis of the male is gripped by the vaginal muscles of the female. The dogs usually stay inextricably locked together for about 15 minutes. When the act is over, the two dogs face in opposite directions. Dousing the animals with cold water or other attempts to separate them by force are cruel. This state of remaining locked together is perfectly natural (see also The Sex Drive in Dogs, page 68).

Crank tail
Low carriage of the tail.

Cross breeding
The deliberate mating of individuals of different breeds, such as Newfoundlands with Saint Bernards, which resulted in the Leonberger breed. Or the mating of different, closely related species, such as the horse and the donkey. Most dog breeds are the result of crossings. Typical examples are the Doberman pinscher and the Airedale terrier. Dog breeders also speak of crossings when unrelated animals of the same breed are mated (outcrossing)

Croup
Rear end of the dog's body.

Cruft's Dog Show 1886
This show, which was named for Charles Cruft in 1886, is the largest dog show in the world. About 10,000 dogs are entered in this show, which is held every February in London.

Cur
Mongrel.

Curly hair
The individual hairs are curled as in a poodle and tend to mat (corded poodles).

Hair that is less curly and thicker is found in Old English sheep dogs (see SHAGGY FUR).

D

Death, sudden
Possible causes:
- internal bleeding caused by a tear in the liver or spleen
- heart failure in large breeds
- twisted stomach in large breeds after consumption of large, heavy meals
- heat stroke
- overexertion; for instance in a hunting dog that lives in the city and is suddenly taken out hunting
- choking to death on a large chunk of meat
- uremia (uremic poisoning) in combination with other strains put on the body at the same time

Dentition
A healthy adult dog has 42 teeth of different shapes, namely the INCISORS, CANINE TEETH, PREMOLARS, and MOLARS. Depending on the breed and the shape of the skull, the teeth meet in different—desirable or undesirable patterns, called bites: the level or pincer bite of wild dogs, the SCISSOR BITE characteristic of most breeds, the UNDERSHOT BITE of boxers and bulldogs, the OVERSHOT BITE sometimes found in dachshunds and greyhounds.

Dewclaw
An extra claw, on the inside of the dog's leg, too high to touch the ground. Dewclaws are digits left over from the evolutionary past. Some large breeds like Saint Bernards and Beaucerons (French herding dogs) sometimes have dewclaws on their hind legs. If not prescribed in the breed's standard, dewclaws on the hind legs are removed surgically during the first few weeks by the breeder. The dewclaws on the front legs are located a couple of inches above the ground and don't get any wear. They should therefore be cut regularly (see page 33). If they grow too long they curl and can get caught in the collar and be torn off. Many breeders remove the front dewclaws when the puppies are young. I am strongly in favor of leaving them alone. They are natural tools the dog uses for manipulating natural or artificial chew bones and when playing with sticks.

Dewlap
Flap of loose skin beneath the throat; also called pendulous skin. Permitted in breeds like Saint Bernards, basset hounds, and bloodhounds.

Displacement activity
A concept from ethology. Inner tensions are released by reactions that have little to do with the actual situation. In dogs, scratching themselves and yawning are examples. Similar to a person's head scratching when confused or embarrassed.

Docking and cropping
Tails are docked and ears cropped to suit the STANDARD of a particular breed.

Dog biscuits
Dog biscuits were first marketed around 1860 by J. Spratt as a special food for dogs. Today dog biscuits are made of cereals and meat meal, to which vitamins and minerals are added. They keep well and are easily digestible as well as nutritious.

Dog breeding
There are no special legal regulations affecting the breeding of dogs. A breeder needs no proof of special training, but anyone who joins a dog club associated with the American Kennel Club has to obey the club's guidelines and breeding rules.

Dog fleas
Dog fleas can also live on humans, just as human fleas can transfer to dogs. The difference between the two can be detected only with the help of a magnifying glass. The dog flea, *Ctenocephalides canis*, is longer than the human flea, *Pulex irritans*, and doesn't jump as well. Flea bites itch and can give rise to allergic reactions. Signs of fleas are red spots with bite marks as well as black dots, which are the fleas' excrement. An infested dog scratches a lot. Fleas stay on a dog only to eat. They retire to the dog's bed or cracks in the floor when they are full. That's why

not only the dog but its bed, too, has to be treated with flea spray or flea powder (available from pet dealers or drug stores; follow directions carefully).

There is also a drug that is rubbed onto the skin in one spot. The drug enters the bloodstream and effectively gets rid of the fleas.

Dog's nature
The sum total of all inborn and acquired traits, physical and psychological; a dog's qualities and abilities—everything, in short, that affects how the dog relates to the world around it. A dog's basic nature is more important for daily life together than all external beauty. See CHARACTER; Breeds, pages 128–166.

Domestication
This word comes from the Latin *domesticus*, which means "having to do with the home." Domestication is the process of taming wild animals so that they can live with humans. The domestication of wolves dates back to the neolithic period, which began about 10,000 years ago. Here are some theories about how the transformation from wolf to domestic dog might have started:
- According to Konrad Lorenz: People and wolves started to hunt together and found this cooperation to be mutually advantageous.
- According to Wolf Herre: Young wolves were kept caged as food reserves. When they showed a talent for guarding the camp, they were no longer killed for eating.
- According to Erik Zimen: Women were the first to domesticate wolves, using young animals as heating pads, as helpers in keeping infants clean (licking them clean, eating feces), and as guards. (Based on observations among the Turkana nomads in the steppes of northern Kenya.)

Dominant
In genetics, "dominant" describes that half of a pair of genes that manifests itself in the individual and suppresses the other gene, which is called RECESSIVE. In schnauzers, the gene for black is dominant; that for pepper and salt, recessive.

Dorsal stripe
A dark stripe running down the back from the nape to the tip of the tail; in pugs, it is called a "trace."

Dreaming
Dogs dream during the deep sleep phase, the so-called REM (rapid eye movement) sleep. Events from waking life are relived in the dreams: Dogs making running motions, wag their tails, and bark in their sleep. As dogs grow older, they tend to run more in their dreams.

Dry
The adjective "dry" is used for lean, muscular dogs with a thin skin that is stretched taut over the body, so that muscles, tendons, and bones are clearly visible underneath. Greyhounds and bullterriers are good examples.

E

Entropion
Eyelids directed abnormally inwards towards the eye.

Estrus
Also called heat. Periods of sexual receptivity in female dogs, occurring usually twice a year, January to March and August to October. There are many exceptions to this timing: Small dogs have a four-month cycle, large dogs, an eight-month cycle. Basenjis go into heat only once a year. There are three phases of estrus:
1. An initial period of about ten days, characterized by spotting or bleeding.
2. The heat proper, lasting about 12 days, during which the bitch is ready to mate.
3. The fading of estrus.
Signs of estrus: Enlargement of the vulva and vagina; the bitch leaves scent marks in the form of small squirts of urine; male dogs, frequently including strangers, display interest in bitches in heat with obtrusive persistence.

Eye teeth
Canine teeth in the upper jaw.

F

Fall
Hair obscuring the facial features.

False pregnancy

A hormonal and behavioral disorder that appears eight to nine weeks after estrus, the time, that is, when an impregnated bitch would give birth. The belly and mammary glands enlarge, and the bitch behaves as if she were nursing puppies. She is reluctant to get off her bed and refuses to leave the apartment. She makes herself a nest and collects shoes or other objects, which she treats as though they were puppies. The condition can be so extreme that the dog may even lactate. This false lactating period, to which female basset hounds are particularly prone, can last up to four weeks. All these symptoms can occur in milder forms. Ask your veterinarian for advice.

It is *not true* that this is merely an "imaginary pregnancy." *Nor is it true* that a dog that has once had puppies is immune to false pregnancies.

FCI

Stands for Fédération Cynologique Internationale. This is an international umbrella organization for dog breeders and owners, founded in 1912 in Belgium and with chapters in 49 countries.

Feathering

A fringe of longer, soft hair on the backside of the legs, on the ears, or on the tail; especially apparent in setters.

Feral dogs

In addition to PARIAH DOGS and shensi dogs, there are a number of truly wild canines that have not yet been scientifically studied. They are small to medium-sized predators with confusing names, such as marten dog, hyena dog, the maned wolf, and kit fox.

Ferociousness

Aggressiveness is inherent in some dogs and arises from a sense of strength. Ferociousness is not restricted to self-defense but can also, through training, be channeled into defending the master (see AGGRESSION and THRESHOLD OF TOLERANCE).

Field of visions

The area a dog can survey without moving its head. Depending on the shape of the skull and the position of the eyes, a dog can survey an angle of 200 to 270 degrees. For humans the angle is only about 100 degrees (see Why Dogs Respond to Movement, page 50).

Flews

The loose lateral parts of the upper lip of a dog are called the flews.

They are called *pendulous* if they hang down as in basset hounds and boxers, or *well filled* if they hug the teeth, as in bullterriers.

Spaniels often suffer from a foul-smelling eczema inside the lower lip near the canine teeth.

Folded ears

Ears with only the tip leaning forward, as in collies, are called semi-erect or SEMI-PRICK EARS. When as much as a third of the ear is folded down, as in the fox terrier, we speak of folded ears. Folded ears are considered a defect in German shepherd dogs. (See DOCKING AND CROPPING.)

Forequarters

Opposite of HINDQUARTERS. The anterior part of the dog, including the chest, shoulders, and front legs and paws.

Form evaluation

Evaluation of dogs at shows for appearance. The ratings are: "excellent," "very good," "good," "passing," and "insufficient." The evaluation is based on the breed STANDARD.

Fringe

See FEATHERING; PLUME.

G

Gaits

Different methods of moving in dogs, such as walking, trotting, loping, and running.

Glaucoma

Increased fluid pressure on the eyeball, usually hereditary. Symptoms include: avoiding of bright light, tearing, and enlarged pupil. Common in some breeds like cocker spaniels, poodles, fox terriers, and basset hounds. Visit the veterinarian if any of these symptoms occurs.

Glow

Red to auburn markings found on dark, usually black, dogs.

Graying

At age six, dogs begin to turn gray around the lips and chin. The gray then spreads across the cheeks and nose. At eight to ten years, white hairs appear around the eyes and, in even older dogs, on the forehead and the rest of the head. Working dogs turn gray earlier than family dogs.

Grizzled

Bluish-gray coloration.

Growling

Usually an indication of discomfort and annoyance but sometimes also an expression of pleasure, as during play. It is a deep humming to rumbling sound.

Guard dogs

Any dog can be trained to bark at or attack potential intruders. However, this role is traditionally assigned to the more powerful breeds, including the following: the German shepherd dog, the boxer, the rottweiler, the Doberman pinscher, the giant schnauzer, the Airedale terrier, the Hovawart, the Bouvier des Flandres, the bullmastiff, and the komondor.

Guard hair

Stiff hairs that stick out beyond the wooly UNDERCOAT.

Gun-barrel front

Rounded chest above very straight forelegs.

H

Harefoot

Long, flat, narrow feet such as those of borzois and Maltese.

Heat

Another expression for ESTRUS.

Heel nipping

This is part of the natural play of young wolves and is retained by some adult dogs. In Appenzell mountain dogs, well-aimed heel nipping is part of their herding work.

Height

The desirable height of a breed is laid down in the STANDARD and is measured with a ruler at the WITHERS, the highest point of the anterior back.

Hindquarters

A term taken over from horse terminology. It refers to the posterior end of a dog, from the hipbone to the hind feet.

Hip dysplasia

A hereditary malformation of the hip joint that occurs in larger dogs. Because of a flattening of the joint socket, the ball of the femur is held too loosely in the pelvic socket. The result is a limp in one or both legs and difficulty in getting up from a sitting position. The symptoms can be alleviated and deterioration halted by proper treatment, but the disease itself is incurable. Breeds susceptible to this condition are: German shepherd dogs, Saint Bernards, Swiss mountain dogs, Newfoundlands, rottweilers, bobtails, boxers, Great Danes, and Labrador retrievers. They are either heavy dogs or ones with sloping backs (German shepherds and boxers). With these dogs it is important to check the family history for hip dysplasia.

Hound

A term designating a hunting dog as opposed to dogs in general. More specifically it includes dogs used in hunting on horseback, like basset hounds, beagles, foxhounds, harriers, otter hounds, and staghounds. In England, basenjis, bloodhounds, elkhounds, the spitz group, and the greyhounds are also placed in this category.

Hunting dogs

Breeds that are suited for hunting. These dogs should be owned only by hunters. That is why in the breed section of this book (pages 128–166) you will find listed only hunting dogs that have become primarily household pets, such as the dachshund, the cocker spaniel, retrievers, and setters. Bloodhounds, pointers, terriers, and other hounds are also considered hunting dogs.

Hunting instinct

A trait, left over from the wolf past of dogs, that is more or less pronounced in different breeds but probably present in all dogs to some degree. That is why you always should keep a dog on a leash in areas where there is hunting.

Hybrid
This is another term for MONGREL.

I

Imprinting
A term used by ethologists to describe permanent impressions received at a very early age. It is important that a puppy be imprinted to *one human* very early so it will later respond the same way to *people in general* (see BOND TO HUMANS).

Inbreeding
Mating of closely related animals. This prevents new genetic defects from arising (no new genes are introduced by unrelated animals), but defects that were present in the gene pool can become manifest. Properly practiced inbreeding allows a breeder to eliminate hereditary defects from breeding lines quickly and thoroughly. Improper inbreeding increases the occurrence of hereditary defects.

Incestuous breeding
Mating of family members, such as brother and sister, mother and son, or father and daughter. It often happens in the wild without ill effects.

Incisors
Teeth between the canines at the front of the mouth.

Insect bites
These are usually harmless, unless they are in the oral cavity, where they can obstruct breathing. In such cases, or if insect bites cause reactions like fever and metabolic disturbances, the dog should be taken to the veterinarian.

Intimidation display
A term from the field of ethology. In dogs, intimidation displays frequently take the form of facial expressions and bodily gestures to establish rank order without having to resort to fighting. Through posture, raising the fur, pricking the ears, and stiffening the tail, a dog tries to make itself look bigger. A dog's bared teeth and growling convey to us humans, too, the impression of danger, with the emphasis on "impression." Fixed staring at the opponent is also part of the intimidation display.

The saying that a dog never attacks anyone who looks it straight in the eye is wrong and can, if followed, provoke an attack from an initially peaceful dog (see page 60).

Invitation to play
This is a typical gesture in the repertoire of canine BODY LANGUAGE. To show that they want to play, not fight, dogs lower the front of the body to the ground while the hind legs remain straight and the tail is raised. The face wears a laughing expression.

Itching
A sensation caused by the nerve ends under the skin. Itching may be a sign of inadequate grooming, too many baths with the wrong soap, fleas (see Dog fleas, page 96) or lice, grass mites (in the summer and fall), ear mites, ticks, allergies, eczema (obvious on the inside of the thighs or on the back), or nephritis.

J

Judge
Judges rate dogs in competitions for appearance and performance. There are judges for individual breeds and those who judge a variety of breeds. The position of a judge presupposes intensive study and training.

K

Kiss marks
Small spotted areas on the face, usually brownish in color.

L

Laxatives, natural
Among these are udder meat, raw liver, lung, raw eggs, and broth made from horse meat.

Lethal factor
Genes that carry serious malformations and sometimes lead to stillbirths. Lethal factors are often connected to desirable breed traits. Thus a white coat (in bull terriers) or the spotted coat of Dalmatians is linked to deafness. Lethal factors can be RECESSIVE and remain undetected. They can become apparent if inbreeding is practiced.

Liability insurance

According to civil law, the owner of an animal is held responsible if the animal causes injury or death to a person or does damage to property. Liability insurance is therefore a must for any dog owner.

License fees

Dogs are the only pets or domestic animals for which the owner has to pay a license fee. Dog owners are required to notify the appropriate office of their community within the locally specified time after acquiring a dog. After paying the license fee, the owner receives a dog tag that the animal must wear whenever it is off the owner's property (see page 23).

Line breeding

The attempt (1) to strengthen desirable traits present in a line or family by mating related dogs and (2) to eliminate less desirable traits by mating individuals in whom these traits are absent. This practice is based on the theory that related animals with an external resemblance must have similar genes.

Litter

All the puppies of one whelping. The number varies from three to ten according to the size of the breed. If there is a very large litter, some of the whelps can be given to a foster mother.

Liver

Dark reddish-brown hair.

Long-haired

Used for dogs with an OUTERCOAT of long, soft hair. Some breeds, like the Newfoundland, also have a good woolly UNDERCOAT. Other long-haired breeds, like the setters, have no woolly undercoat or—like the Maltese—only a thin, silky one. If the undercoat is thick and the hairs of the outer coat stick out straight, as in the spitz group, we speak of long guard hair.

M

Markings

Patches of brown, gray, black, or other colors on the head or body of a white or other-colored dog. Examples of dogs with markings are basset hounds and Swiss mountain dogs. The markings can also be in a flecked or marbled or tiger pattern, as in the pointer.

Mask

A sharply delineated foreface that differs in color from the rest of the face. Mastiffs and pugs have masks (black), as do border collies and some terriers.

Modification

Deviations from the physical norm, such as in size, that are caused by external factors. Environmental influences play a crucial role here.

Molars

Back teeth with flattened surfaces.

Mongrel

Offspring of parents of different breeds.

Mutation

Changes, both external and internal, that appear spontaneously. These changes are passed on to future generations because they originate in the genes. The reasons mutations occur are still unknown.

Mutt

See MONGREL.

Muzzle

1. The front of a dog's face, including the nose and jaws. The shape of the muzzle depends on the dog's breed. 2. A covering for the dog's face, to prevent eating or biting.

N

Naming dogs

The official name of a purebred dog consists of two parts: the puppy's own name and the name of the kennel. Breeders have to follow these rules:

1. All the names of the puppies of one litter have to start with the same letter.

2. These initial letters have to be used in alphabetical order for successive litters. Fanfan, Fidel, Flora, and Fussy thus would all be puppies of the sixth litter born in a given kennel. This rule had the effect that most dogs are not called by the names that are listed in their registration papers.

Neoteny
State of arrested development that persists into sexual maturity. In dogs this is a consequence of domestication. This concept from ethology has found expression in the following catchy statement: Dogs are wolves at an immature stage of development, and humans are immature apes.

Nose leather
The fleshy tip of a dog's nose, usually black, in health always wet, often aquiver. The skin is puckered and the nose looks like a truffle or a huge berry. (See also Nose contact, page 58).

Novice class (official show class)
Open to dogs six months of age or older that have never won a first prize in any class other than puppy class, and fewer than three first prizes in the novice class itself. Limited to dogs whelped in the United States or Canada.

Nudging with the nose
During puppyhood this is a begging gesture addressed to the mother, asking her to share some of the food in her mouth. In grown dogs it is a greeting or, combined with licking, a gesture of affection. If a strange dog sniffs you, you can hold out the back of your hand and lightly tap the dog's nose. This is a human substitute for nose nudging and is understood as such by normal dogs.

Nursing period
A mother dog nurses her pups for five to eight weeks. During the first two weeks usually no additional food is necessary.

Nutritionally complete diet
The desire to feed our pets as healthy a diet as possible is a phenomenon of our time. Such a diet for dogs means commercial dog food. A good definition of a nutritionally complete diet is one which provides everything needed by the animal to sustain itself and to reproduce itself. See Dogs and their diet, pages 87–93.

O

Obese Dogs
Excess weight is shed only slowly. If you give your dog 60 percent of its normal ration, it will lose 2 percent of its body weight per week. A good alternative to enforced fasting is to stimulate the metabolism by feeding the dog once a week some sour milk with half a day-old roll (see also Special Diets for Dogs, page 91).

Olfactory area
The part of a dog's nose that has olfactory cells. This area is 30 times as large in dogs as in humans. No wonder dogs have such a sharp sense of smell (see A Dog's Nose, page 49).

Open class (official show class)
Open to dogs six months of age or over, with no exceptions.

Outercoat
What the coat of dogs originally was like. It consists of a dense undercoat and medium long guard hairs, as in the German shepherd dog.

Overbreeding
When breeders try too hard to achieve certain goals like size, emphasis on individual body parts, or general appearance, this can result in physical defects and mental degeneration, such as abnormal behavior (see BREED DEFECTS).

Overshot bite
The lower jaw is too short so that the teeth of the upper jaw come down in front of the lower incisors when the mouth is shut. An overshot bite is not desirable but occurs in breeds with long skulls, such as greyhounds, dachshunds, and spaniels.

P

Pads
Tough, leathery areas on the feet that are devoid of hair.

Panting
Rapid breathing with open mouth and with the tongue hanging out to cool the body down by evaporation. Panting is a kind of substitute for sweating since dogs have only minimal sweat glands on the pads of their feet.

Pariah Dogs
Found from the Balkans to southern Asia, these "street" dogs live, often in groups,

near human settlements; each group has its own leader, the king pariah. It is unclear whether they are feral descendants of ancient breeds or dogs at an early stage of DOMESTICATION. The Canaan dog of Israel is considered a breed and there is even a standard for it.

Pawing the ground
Pawing the ground after urinating is a sign of social standing and not directed at any particular dog. Often seen in small dogs. Pawing and scratching can also be a DISPLACEMENT ACTIVITY.

Pedigree
A visual representation in the shape of a tree or a table of a dog's ancestors. The term pedigree is often loosely and mistakenly used instead of REGISTRATION PAPERS when people refer to a dog's breed certification.

Pepper and salt
Descriptive term for an OUTERCOAT of dark hairs with white tips, as in schnauzers.

Phenotype
The external appearance of an individual dog. It is a result of nature and nurture, that is, a combination of inherited traits (genotype) and external influences.

Pigmentation
Accumulation of pigments on the skin of the eyelids, the nose leather, and the edges of the lips. Not desirable in white dogs.

Plume
A fringe of long hair hanging from the underside of the tail.

Pregnancy
The average pregnancy or gestation period lasts 63 days in dogs (see page 70).

Premolars
Teeth between the molars and CANINE TEETH.

Pricked ears
Erect ears; in the past cropping was used to help the ears of some breeds stay erect. Natural pricked ears sometimes take six months or more to become erect. Among the breeds that have natural pricked ears

are the German shepherd dog, the chow chow, the spitz group, the Samoyed, the basenji, and the bullterrier. Schnauzers, pinschers, Dobermans, and Great Danes have cropped pricked ears.

Pulse
You can feel a dog's pulse on the inside of the thigh near the groin. A normal pulse rate for large to medium-sized dogs is 70 to 100; for smaller breeds, 100 to 130; and for puppies, up to 200 beats per minute.

Puppy class
Open to dogs at least six months and not more than twelve months of age. Limited to dogs whelped in the United States and Canada.

Purebred
Bred from members of a recognized breed over many generations. A dog from a good kennel has its background documented by its PEDIGREE and is purebred. Purebred does not mean uniformity of genetic material, when all offspring would be clones of their parents.

Q

Quarantine
Temporary isolation of sick animals or ones suspected of harboring a contagious disease, to prevent epidemics. Because of the danger of RABIES, all dogs entering or leaving England, Norway, and Sweden have to undergo several weeks of quarantine. (The word comes from the French and originally designated a period of 40 days).

R

Rabies
Serious acute disease, caused by the virus *Formido inexoribilis*, transmitted by infected saliva, most often by biting. Among the symptoms are raging behavior and inability to swallow despite extreme thirst; hydrophobia (fear of water) is a misnomer. Vaccination of every dog is needed to break the chain of infection.

Recessive
The opposite of DOMINANT. Genetic traits that are hidden but are passed on to future

generations, where they may manifest themselves.

Registration Papers
Record on an official form issued, in the United States, by the American Kennel Club or, in Great Britain, by the English Kennel Club and stating that both parents of a puppy were purebred dogs of the breed in question. The registration papers are signed by an official of the appropriate breed club and by the BREEDER. Usually the breeder registers the litter as a whole, and it is up to the owner to register the puppy separately, which is done by filling out an application and sending it, along with a fee, to the appropriate address. The club then issues a certificate of registration. This certificate usually includes an exact description of the dog and a pedigree going back at least three generations. Also, wrongly, called a PEDIGREE.

Reliable
The quality of a dog that feels secure and is not easily upset (see also THRESHOLD OF TOLERANCE).

Ringtail
A curled tail carried high over the back or sideways. Pugs, Japanese spaniels, and Pekinese have ringtails, as do all members of the spitz group. Ringtails are a sign of DOMESTICATION.

Roached back
Specialized term for a strongly curved back, which is generally considered a defect. In bulldogs, Italian greyhounds, and whippets it is considered a trait of the breed. Also called carp back.

Roaming
Unsupervised and illegal wandering. Male dogs are more inclined to roam. If a dog goes roaming even though it is taken on regular walks, this is a sign of poor training or disturbed behavior.

Rolling
Dogs have a special interest in things that offend our noses. The more "civilized" a dog's life and food, the greater its pleasure in rolling in anything that smells bad. Dogs like to "perfume" themselves, particularly the head, neck, and shoulders.

Rose ears
Ears with the flap folded back and the tip hanging down so as to reveal part of the ear BURR. Examples: English bulldogs, greyhounds, and whippets.

Rudder
A dog's tail.

Ruff
The area of long hair around the neck of a chow chow.

S

Scenting the air
Dogs raise their noses into the wind to pick up scent particles present in the air. This shows how acute their sense of smell is.

Scent mark
A tiny squirt of urine with which a male dog "marks" its territory and attempts to cover up scent marks left behind by other dogs. This is the reason why male dogs lift their legs so frequently.

Scissor bite
In the scissor bite the INCISORS of the upper jaw close over those of the lower jaw somewhat like scissors closing. This DENTITION is desirable in almost all breeds.

Selective breeding
Under normal conditions a breeder selects those animals for reproduction that exhibit the qualities considered desirable. In this fashion the breeder can influence the quality of a breed for the better or the worse.

The natural selection taking place among wild animals favors the stronger males, which are more likely than weaker ones to win a female and thus pass on their traits to future generations. Among wolves, it is only the ALPHA ANIMALS that reproduce.

Self-colored
Single colored.

Semi-prick ears
Like FOLDED EARS but with only the very tip of the ear folded forward, as in collies and shelties.

Sense of orientation
Dogs have the ability, not yet explained by

science, to find their way home over long distances.

Shaggy fur
Very long, coarse hair, such as the fur of Old English sheep dogs. Sometimes tends to get matted, as in komondors and pulis.

Shaking
All dogs are experts at shaking themselves to get every muscle and tendon, indeed the whole body, back into perfect shape after waking up. It is a skill we all could benefit from if we acquired it. When old or sick dogs no longer shake after getting up, this is a bad sign concerning their overall state of health.

Shaking paws
This trick goes back to the original begging gesture which puppies that are still blind use when they push (or knead) with their paws against their mother's teats. Our dogs have learned to modify the gesture and use it to say "Please, please."

Shedding
In moderate climates dogs shed twice a year. How much they shed depends on their living conditions and diet. During the shedding period, grooming—that is, brushing and combing—is especially important (see page 32).

Shensi dogs
Primitive tropical dogs that exist independent of humans. About 15 different types have been described, among them the Batak spitz of Sumatra, the Papua dog of New Guinea, the Cameroon dog, and the pygmy dog. The basenji is recognized as a breed by the AKC. Each of these primitive tropical dogs has PRICKED EARS and a RINGTAIL.

Short-haired
Used for dogs with an OUTERCOAT made up of very short hairs that lie down close to the body over an almost nonexistent wooly UNDERCOAT. Examples are short-haired pointers, boxers, Dobermans, and some dachshunds and fox terriers.

Shows
See CAC, CACIB, CACIT

Size of dogs
Dogs are classified by size into four groups:
- *Toy dogs* measure at most 9½ inches (24 cm) at the WITHERS.
- *Miniature dogs* measure up to 16 inches (41 cm) at the WITHERS.
- *Medium-sized dogs* measure up to 24½ inches (62 cm) at the WITHERS.
- *Large dogs* are over 24½ inches (62 cm) at the WITHERS.

Sleep
Sleep is as important for dogs as food. Physical deterioration caused by exhaustion can quickly lead to death. Dogs doze during the day, which means that they drop off into a deep sleep within seconds but also become wide awake within an instant. There is no reason to worry if your dog spends 20 out of 24 hours dozing and sleeping; this is not a sign of ill health.

Smooth coat
See SHORT-HAIRED.

Splay foot
Toes kept wide apart.

Standard
Description of an ideal dog of a given breed, including all the required traits. The standard is made up by the national club responsible for the breed in question and submitted to the FCI, which sends copies to all the member national organizations so that breeds will be judged uniformly. The form used universally for breed standards was drafted at the Congress of Cynologists at Monaco.

Stop
A pronounced step up from the MUZZLE to the forehead. Salukis and Afghans have hardly any stop, while boxers, Pekingese, and Japanese spaniels have very big ones.

Strain
A group of dogs belonging to the same breed that share some additional trait, such as size (light strain, heavy strain) or color.

Stroking
Puppies as well as adult dogs have a need

to be stroked. Puppies want the physical closeness with their mother, and later on dogs crave the touch of the human hand. Some dogs keep asking to be petted by NUDGING WITH THE NOSE or scratching to the point of becoming a nuisance. Others are more restrained. Petting and stroking should not be too rough and should extend beyond the head and shoulder region. Placing one's flat hand on a dog's belly has an incredibly calming effect. Dogs also love to be scratched near the base of the tail (see page 65).

Stud book

Stud books are kept by the breed clubs. All registered purebred dogs are entered into them, and they are an important source of information on the history of the breed. However, the defects of individual dogs are not entered. The PEDIGREE of a dog that cannot be verified in the stud book is worthless.

T

Tan

A yellowish to orange-brown color, as in black and tan terriers.

Tattooing

A way of marking the STUD BOOK number on the puppies of some breeds. The number is tattooed into the ear or on the inside of the thigh. Tattooed letter or number combinations also help identify lost, stolen, and abandoned dogs.

Threshold of tolerance

The magnitude of an external stimulus required to elicit a reaction. The threshold of tolerance varies from breed to breed, depends on the animal's sex, is affected by early experiences, and may vary depending on the situation. Dogs with a low threshold of tolerance respond with aggressive behavior to minute stimuli, while dogs with a high threshold remain calm and relaxed. Breeds characterized by a high threshold include the Saint Bernard, the Bouvier des Flandres, the bullterrier, and the Tibetan mastiff. The standard for the Fila Brasileiro prescribes a low threshold, which I consider foolish as well as frivolous.

Ticks

A parasite, *Ixodes ricinus*, that is a fraction of an inch long when hungry and attaches itself to the skin of dogs or people, where it sucks itself full of blood until it is round like a pea. Then the female tick (only the female sucks blood) drops to the ground. The bite causes a strong itch.

How to remove ticks: Dab with alcohol, oil, or tick oil, wait about ten minutes, then carefully pull the tick from the skin with tweezers. Make sure you remove the entire animal, including mouth and pincers. Tourists have introduced the brown tick (*Rhipicephalis sanguineus*) into the U.S.A. This thrives only in temperatures above 68°F (20°C), but it's dangerous because it is a carrier of meningitis. Ask your veterinarian if there are brown ticks in your area.

Toy breeds

Tiny dogs of normal growth and even proportions. Not to be confused with pathologically inhibited growth (nanism). Quite a few breeds are bred in toy size.

Trials

Tests for hunting and guard dogs set up by various breed clubs. Dogs that pass the trials are awarded a certificate.

Tulip ears

Pointed PRICKED EARS resembling the petals of a tulip, as in the Skye terrier, the Scotch terrier, or the German shepherd dog.

Turning in circles

Turning several times in a circle before lying down is not an instinctive action but rather a way to get the spine ready for the usually curled up sleeping posture. This circling goes back to the dogs' early wild past when the tall grass had to be stamped down to make a bed.

U

Undercoat

Woolly hair underneath the topcoat. This undercoat protects the dog against cold in the winter and against the rays of the sun in the summer. Many breeds have some undercoat, but sled dogs and Landseers have particularly thick ones.

Undershot bite

The INCISORS of the lower jaw project beyond those of the upper jaw without touching them when the mouth closes. Accepted in boxers, bulldogs, pugs, and Pekinese; considered a defect in other breeds.

V

Vegetarian food

Vegetarian food can occasionally be beneficial for dogs, but in the long run it is inadequate because dogs are carnivores (see Dogs and Their Diet, page 87).

V-shaped

FOLDED EARS whose folded tip looks like the letter V. Fox terriers have such ears.

W

Wavy hair

The hairs of both the OUTERCOAT and the UNDERCOAT are wavy, as in the borzoi. If the hair is very wavy, it is considered CURLY HAIR.

Whelp

A puppy from the time it is born until all its milk teeth have grown in. At 3½ to 4 months the milk teeth begin to be replaced by the permanent ones.

Wirehaired

Describes a coat of rough, short or medium-long hairs that feel wiry to the touch and stick out in all directions. Wirehaired dachshunds and various terriers are examples.

Withers

The part of the spine that lies between the shoulder blades but does not rise above them. The height of a dog is measured there (see HEIGHT).

Y

Young dog

Appropriate term for a dog up to 18 months old but no longer a puppy.

Breeds: Profiles of Popular Purebred Dogs

In this section I present in pictures and words dog breeds ranging from the Great Dane to the dachshund. These profiles give you important information on the dogs' appearance, how they should be kept, what their character and specific qualities are, and what ailments to watch out for.

Specialized terms in the descriptions are explained in the Glossary (pages 112–127).

How to Choose a Breed

The breed's appearance should appeal to you; you may also be drawn to certain character traits in one breed or another. But make sure you compare your wishes with reality. Ask yourself whether your dream dog will fit in with your living situation and life-style. Your dog should not be "one size too big" and should not weigh more than you do. There are situations where you would be unable to cope with such a big animal.

To start, you may want to consider the breeds that are the most popular in the United States. They are:

1. Cocker spaniel
2. Poodle
3. Labrador retriever
4. German shepherd dog
5. Golden retriever
6. Doberman pinscher
7. Beagle
8. Chow chow
9. Miniature schnauzer
10. Shetland sheep dog

Selecting a dog is more crucial than deciding what kind of car to buy. If you get a car that turns out to be too big or too small, or too expensive to run, it can be replaced. The same is not true with a dog. Once it has placed its trust and affections in a master to whom alone it subordinates itself, accepting this person as its superior and the leader of the pack, a dog would suffer deeply if it were separated from its people and would find it hard to accept a new master.

Before you choose a rare breed you should do some research. Rare breeds have a small genetic breeding pool, and positive breeding results depend very much on individual animals. You should familiarize yourself with the family history of the dogs and also find out if there are ailments or defects that typically occur in the breed. Visit the kennels where the dogs you are interested in are bred, and get all the literature you can find.

The appearance and characteristics of a breed are described in the breed's standard (see Glossary, STANDARD). The standard is drawn up by the breed's club and formally accepted by the Fédération Cynologique International (FCI) and the American Kennel Club (AKC) after which the standard has international validity. My descriptions are based on those in the breed standards.

Note: Almost all the pictures published in this section were taken especially for this book. Most of the dogs depicted were recommended by the particular clubs as handsome representatives of their breed and conforming to their standards.

Opposite page: A very prominent dog. "Uran von Wilderteiger Land": World Champion of German Sheperd Dog Club in 1985 and of the German Kennel Club in 1987.

Great Dane

Doberman

A giant animal with a long history, the Great Dane is called the "Apollo among dogs" by its breeders.

Height, weight: Males at least 31½ inches (80 cm) at the shoulders, providing he is well proportioned to his height; the females should not be less than 28 inches (71 cm) at the shoulders, but it is preferable that she be 30 inches (76 cm) or more, providing she is well proportioned to her height. 187 pounds (85 kg) and over.
Coat and color: Short, thick, smooth, glossy. Five colors: Fawn, brindle, black and white harlequin, black, and blue.
Appearance: Noble and distinguished, with an expressive head.
Suitable for: People who know dogs and have plenty of room.
Not suitable for: Beginners and people with cluttered living space.
Requirements: Needs its own room and consistent training.
Grooming: Needs very little.
Qualities as a family member: An affectionate dog that doesn't bark much. Good watchdog. Suspicious of strangers.
Breed character: Self-confident, aloof, not a fighter. Quiet, sensitive, good with children.
Problems associated with breed: Many people are afraid of all Great Danes. Proper training is best achieved by taking obedience courses.
Ailments associated with breed: Twisted stomach after hasty eating; cardiac weakness.
Life expectancy: Medium.
Daily caloric needs: Up to 4,575 calories.
Remarks: This dream dog (for most dog lovers) has always been a prestige dog, but please don't get one as a status symbol.
Picture: Brindle bitch, 2½ years old.

A German breed with a "dangerous" look. Strong and muscular, very fast, and an incorruptible watchdog.

Height, weight: Males up to 27½ inches (70 cm); females between 24 to 26 inches (61–66 cm), ideal about 27½ inches (70 cm); up to 57 pounds (26 kg). Very elegant look.
Coat and color: Short, hard, and thick. Black, brown, or blue with sharply defined rust-red markings.
Appearance: Has a poker face that makes it hard to read its moods.
Suitable for: Sports enthusiasts or people who want an effective watchdog.
Not suitable for: People who don't engage in any sport, don't have quick physical reactions, and don't like to have a bodyguard around.
Requirements: Needs very solid training, plenty of exercise, and work. Can spend part of the time outdoors.
Grooming: Needs very little.
Qualities as a family member: Devoted to its family and to children.
Breed character: Spirited, fearless, self-assured, naturally aggressive, sensitive.
Problems associated with breed: Because of breeders' overemphasis on physical appearance there are dangerous Dobermans in whom aggressiveness predominates.
Ailments associated with breed: Loss of hair; not prone to hip dysplasia!
Life expectancy: Up to 14 years.
Daily caloric needs: 1,480 calories.
Remarks: Belongs to the pinscher family and was named (1860) for Louis Dobermann who developed the breed. Typical one-person dog.
Picture: Black male, two years old.

Afghan

Saluki

Extremely attractive Oriental dog that sometimes feels it is equal to humans. Close to nature but enjoys comfort.

Height, weight: Males about 27½ inches (70 cm); bitches 25 inches (63½ cm); up to 66 pounds (30 kg). A dog that makes people stop and admire it.
Coat and color: Strikingly long, silky hair. All colors permitted.
Appearance: With its spectacular coat it looks almost too elegant for a dog.
Suitable for: Devoted fanciers who are sensitive to their dog's needs.
Not suitable for: People who are not willing to pay tribute to their dog's beauty by dedicating time and energy to grooming every day.
Requirements: Needs a long daily run and one person to whom it can form a lifelong attachment.

Grooming: Careful combing and brushing.
Qualities as a family member: Obedient and watchful. Not easy to keep.
Breed character: Wins admirers through its dignity and calm and pleasant nature. Afghans love their own people but are cool toward strangers.
Problems associated with breed: Its past as a hunting dog reasserts itself periodically. Since Afghans hunt by sight they should always be kept on a leash outdoors.
Ailments associated with breed: Not much known.
Life expectancy: Normal.
Daily caloric needs: For a dog of 62 pounds (28 kg), 1,650 calories.
General remarks: Legend has it that Noah took Afghan hounds on his ark. This gives some idea of the antiquity of the breed.
Picture: In front, red male, 15 months old; in back, blue male, two years old.

The prototype of an Oriental greyhound. Light, agile and fast, quick to learn and intelligent, eager for its master's praise.

Height, Weight: 23½ to 27½ inches (60–70 cm); bitches may be considerably smaller, this being typical of the breed; 31 to 55 pounds (14–25 kg). Handsome, graceful, almost delicate.
Coat: Silky-haired with feathering or smooth-haired without feathering.
Appearance: What is striking is the profound, strangely sad expression of the beautiful, almond-shaped eyes.
Suitable for: Fanciers who can offer this dog a lot of opportunity for running.
Not suitable for: People who want a fancy dog merely to show off.
Requirements: Needs a lot of affection. Not a dog for children.
Grooming: Needs little.

Qualities as a family member: A quiet, gentle, and dignified dog that becomes attached to one person. Can be trained only with love and consistency.
Breed character: Quiet indoors, active outside. Is happiest when running.
Problems associated with breed: Cannot bear harsh discipline or strictness; cringing obedience is foreign to it. Is not easy to keep.
Ailments associated with breed: Not much known.
Life expectancy: Normal.
Daily caloric needs: For a dog weighing 44 pounds (20 kg), 1,250 calories.
Remarks: Native in the area from Turkey to eastern Turkestan; the dog of the nomadic bedouin. Runs like a dream, barely touching the ground. Racing speeds up to 35 mph (55 km/h).
Picture: Grizzle and tan bitch, three years old.

German Shepherd Dog

A dog described by superlatives: the world's most valued working dog; the best known breed.

Height, weight: 25½ inches (62.5 cm); bitches 22 to 24 inches (56–61 cm). The length is measured from the point of the breastbone to the rear of the pelvis; 66 to 77 pounds (30–35 kg). It should be clear at a glance if a dog is a male or a female.

Coat and color: Double coat with a dense outer coat and a thick, bushy tail. Black, with yellow to light gray markings.

Appearance: Expressive head with beautiful, intelligent eyes. Well-proportioned body that is harmonious in all its movements. Cannot be mistaken for any other dog.

Suitable for: People who want a dog willing to subordinate itself and who are able to spend two hours a day working with the dog. Also people who need a watchdog and who are energetic.

Not suitable for: Older, delicate, or less energetic people who live in small apartments. This is not a dog that stays "under the couch" or even "on the couch," nor can it be kept outdoors all the time.

Requirements: German shepherds need regular training sessions, plenty of exercise, and thorough training.

Grooming: A thorough daily brushing, especially during shedding season. One or two baths per year.

Qualities as a family member: Exceptionally good watchdog, sometimes given to barking. Loves to be close to its family. Watch out in hunting areas; German shepherds tend to chase game.

Breed character: Eager to learn and eager to subordinate itself to a master. Courageous as well as sensitive; average temperament. Less sensitive individual dogs need a firm hand.

Problems associated with breed: Improperly trained dogs or ones with an unreliable character (from unplanned matings) tend to be fighters that bite even small dogs and bitches.

Ailments associated with breed: When buying a puppy, make sure neither parent is afflicted with hip dysplasia (introduced into some lines through emphasis on a sloping back line). Some dogs are neurotically timid. May get diabetes in old age.

Life expectancy: High, up to 14 years.

Daily caloric needs: For a dog weighing 66 pounds (30 kg), 1,700 calories; for a 70-pound (32 kg) animal, 1,820 calories.

Remarks: The German Shepherd Club of Germany was founded in 1899 by Max Emil Friedrich von Stephanitz, who saw to it that the breed did not become a fad or a status symbol. Clubs throughout the world have continued to adhere to the same high principles.

Picture: Black male with red and brown markings, 6½ years old.

Collie

Long-haired Scottish sheepdog of great beauty. Became fashionable twice within a hundred years: first under Queen Victoria, later because of Lassie.

Height, weight: Males up to 26 inches (66 cm) at the shoulder; bitches are from 22 to 24 inches (56–61 cm) at the shoulder; up to 75 pounds (34 kg). Long body with deep chest.

Coat and color: Long, thick, and harsh to the touch; the smooth variety has a short, thick coat. Tan and white, tricolor (black, white and tan), and blue merle.

Appearance: Made immortal by Lassie. Very attractive.

Suitable for: People who love beauty and also have enough leisure for time-consuming grooming and money for good dog food.

Not suitable for: People who are not interested in a real dog but want a Lassie that acts in accordance with human reasoning.

Requirements: Needs plenty of room and extensive exercise, such as running along next to a bicycle. A collie that is forced to live indoors languishes. Likes company. Not a dog for the city or for high-rise apartment buildings.

Grooming: Combing and brushing take about 15 minutes a day.

Qualities as a family member: Always wants to be with its family and demands attention from its people. Good with children (though not like Lassie). Watchful, barks at anything unusual. Sheds a lot and carries dirt indoors in rainy weather.

Breed character: Aloof, not a dog for everyone. Suspicious toward strangers. Learns easily and is obedient. Psychologically sensitive.

Problems associated with breed: If overbred, dogs can become nervous, hysterical, and even vicious. Can be made neurotic by improper (harsh) training. Be especially careful when choosing the kennel from which to buy a puppy.

Ailments associated with breed: Abnormalities of the eyes and problems with vision. A syndrome called the "collie eye anomaly" can lead to a detached retina. There is also the so-called "collie-nose," an eczema on the unpigmented surface of the nose, caused by exposure to the sun.

Life expectancy: High. Collies can live up to 15 years.

Daily caloric needs: For a dog weighing 55 pounds (25 kg), 1,480 calories.

Remarks: The above descriptions apply to the smooth collie, too, except for the coat texture. The smooth collie is rarer because it doesn't look as attractive as its long-haired cousin. The family also includes the *bearded collie*, which might be taken by the nonexpert for an Old English sheep dog; the *border collie*, a black and white sheep dog; and the *sheltie*, a miniature version from the Shetland Islands, which is also the home of ponies and sheep that are smaller than most (see page 139).

Picture: In front, tan and white bitch, 14 months old; in back, five-year-old tricolor male.

Old English Sheepdog (Bobtail)

Chow chow

The Old English Sheepdog looks as though it stepped out of a Scottish legend. A dog of great charm.

Height, weight: About 22 inches (56 cm); 75 to 88 pounds (34–40 kg). Looks compact.

Coat and color: Shaggy and stringy, no curls, with waterproof undercoat. All shades of gray, grizzle, and blue.

Appearance: Unusual because the body's build and the face can only be guessed at underneath the thick, long fur.

Suitable for: People who know for sure that a bobtail is what they want and who are fully aware of what caring for these dogs entails.

Not suitable for: People who like to give orders or who live in small apartments.

Requirements: Needs lots of space, lots of exercise, and lots of love and affection.

Grooming: A thorough daily brushing and combing (takes about 30 minutes).

Qualities as a family member: Is very much part of the family but also wants some time alone.

Breed character: Spirited, good-natured, adaptable, but also proud and independent.

Problems associated with breed: Not a dog for a fussy housekeeper; the long, thick coat picks up lots of dirt.

Ailments associated with breed: Watch out for hip dysplasia. Otherwise not much known.

Life expectancy: High.

Daily caloric needs: For a dog weighing 77 pounds (35 kg), 1,960 calories.

Remarks: The bobtail's voice sounds like a cracked bell. When walking, the dog looks plump; when running, elegant.

Picture: On the left, five-year-old male; on the right, two-year-old bitch.

A proud, almost lionlike dog with a dignified gait and the look of an individualist.

Height weight: Minimum: 18 inches (45.5 cm); 44 to 55 pounds (20–25 kg). Very compact body.

Coat and color: Abundant, dense. Solid black, red, blue, cinnamon, cream, or white.

Appearance: Fierce and imposing.

Suitable for: People who enjoy a dog with a will of its own and who know how to deal with it.

Not suitable for: People who expect unconditional obedience from a dog.

Requirements: Normal living quarters, but can also live outdoors. Likes to attach itself to one person.

Grooming: Thorough daily coat care.

Qualities as a family member: Attentive watchdog, very quiet. Doesn't need a huge amount of exercise.

Breed character: Self-willed to the point of obstinacy. A one-person dog. Cannot be trained to perform. Unmoved by flattery.

Problems associated with breed: Unhappy when separated from the person it has accepted. Sensitive to heat. Sheds heavily.

Ailments associated with breed: Tends to get eczema. Often suffers from entropion, a turning inward of the eyelid margin, which rubs against the cornea.

Life expectancy: High.

Daily caloric needs: For a dog weighing 50 pounds (23 kg), 1,400 calories.

Remarks: The greatest individualist among dogs. Strong fighter; not a dog for children.

Picture: Red male, six years old.

Saint Bernard

A legend of a dog. A ponderous giant that fascinates children. But don't let them approach and pet this dog unless you know it.

Height, weight: Males up to 27½ inches (70 cm); females 25½ inches (65 cm); bitches are of finer and more delicate build; about 175 pounds (80 kg). Muscular body with massive head.
Coat and color: Medium-long, straight to slightly wavy; in short-haired variety, short and very dense. White with red, red with white, the red in various shades. Feet, chest, and tip of tail always white.
Appearance: Majestic; imposing by its mere presence.
Suitable for: People with lots of space (a country place) and an appreciation for monumental size.
Not suitable for: People who don't admire large size or who think all Saint Bernards are by definition cooperative and sweet-tempered.
Requirements: Not a dog for the city. Needs large quantities of good food. Can be kept outdoors but needs to feel part of the family. Best transported in a station wagon.
Grooming: The longer-haired variety takes time to brush and comb; short-haired Saint Bernards need little grooming.
Qualities as a family member: Good watchdog; fantastic with children; not very noisy. Not too fond of exercise, though it can be trained to enjoy walks. Sensitive and very affectionate. Can knock a person over in an excited welcome.
Breed character: Tranquil and almost phlegmatic, good-natured. Is fearless and has plenty of fighting spirit and toughness. Learns easily. Some lines tend to be aggressive.
Problems associated with breed: Animals from some kennels are too heavy and can hardly move. Puppies should not climb stairs because going down stairs can lead to torn ligaments.
Ailments associated with breed: On the whole hardy but tends to have skin problems, suffer from extropion (folding outward of the eyelid rim, usually on the lower lid) and hip dysplasia. Watch out for twisted stomach.
Life expectancy: About ten years.
Daily caloric needs: For a dog weighing about 150 pounds (68 kg), 3,775 calories; for a 175-pound (80 kg) animal, 4,312 calories. This is more than a man doing hard physical labor needs.
Remarks: Saint Bernards had their great day in history in the early nineteenth century when the hospice at the Great St. Bernard pass in Switzerland used them to rescue people from the snow. The dogs did not acquire their present name until 1865, when fanciers not connected with the hospice began to concentrate on purity of breed. In the early 1870s Saint Bernards were in high fashion, and people paid enormous sums for this dog. The most famous Saint Bernard was Barry, who is said to have saved the lives of over 40 people between 1800 and 1814.
Picture: Four-year-old bitch.

Boxer

A muscular dog with the body of a decathlon athlete. A valiant protector and defender. Always ready to play, even into old age. An ideal family dog.

Height, weight: Males: 22½ to 25 inches (57–63.5 cm); females: 21 inches (53 cm) and up. Weight depending on size, about 66 pounds (30 kg). Large-boned, square build.

Coat and color: Short and shiny, hard to the touch, lying close to the body. Dark fawn to tan, with medium shades most valued; also brindled. Black mask covering muzzle only.

Appearance: A bundle of muscles, loaded with energy. Because of the sloped back line the animal looks ready for action—like a coiled spring. Ferocious facial expression.

Suitable for: A family of sports lovers living in generous quarters, preferably with children.

Not suitable for: People who like and own breakable knick-knacks or who are themselves frail or delicate. Also sedentary people and old people.

Requirements: Needs space—at least a good-sized apartment. Also regular exercise, perhaps running alongside a bicycle, and a daily play session that may entail some rough play. It is a good idea to work with this dog, which is one of the recognized working breeds.

Grooming: Needs very little.

Qualities as a family member: Good watchdog and family dog; loves children. Pleasant though boisterous housemate. Has to be trained with firmness and much praise.

Breed character: Physically as well as mentally robust. Intelligent, easily guided through consistent training. Full of fire and courage. Loves physical affection and remains playful into old age.

Problems associated with breed: Not always friendly toward other dogs. Sometimes tends to pick fights. Drools at the slightest excitement.

Ailments associated with breed: Stiffening of the spine with advanced age. From age eight on more likely to get cancer than other breeds. Tendency to allergies and sometimes subject to hip dysplasia.

Life expectancy: About ten years.

Daily caloric needs: A dog weighing 66 pounds (30 kg) needs 1,696 calories.

Remarks: What is the origin of the breed's name? Was it chosen because of the dog's pushed-in face? Or because this dog fights with its front feet like a boxer? Nobody knows. In any case, the dog and its name found favor, and today boxers are highly popular. The picture on the left shows a dog with uncropped ears.

Picture, left: Male, red and gold brindle, ten months old.

Picture, right: Fawn colored bitch, six years old.

Irish Wolfhound

This gray giant of the Emerald Isle is the world's biggest dog. When it puts its paws on a man's shoulders, it looks down on the man's head.

Height, weight: Males: About 32 inches (81 cm); weight: 110 pounds (50 kg); bitches 30 inches (76 cm); numbers apply only to hounds over 18 months of age. This breed should weigh significantly less than a Great Dane. Strong, imposing build.
Coat and color: Rough and hard on the body, legs, and head and longer but especially hard above the eyes and on lower jaw. Gray, brindle, red, black, pure white, and fawn.
Appearance: Elegant and fear-inspiring to some who are not dog lovers. An unusual kind of dog.
Suitable for: Even-tempered people with enough land and money to offer this dog the kind of life and food it needs.

Not suitable for: City dwellers who want to attract attention by owning an unusual looking dog. Not a dog for a beginner.
Requirements: The size of the dog alone will limit who can keep one. It needs especially large amounts of good food for the first 18 months. Should have extensive daily runs next to a bicycle or horseback rider, but not on a leash.
Grooming: Daily grooming with a metal comb and a hard brush. Loves to be out in wet weather and brings lots of dirt into the house.
Qualities as a family member: A pleasant member of the household that doesn't take up so much room indoors because its movements are calm and controlled. Good manners are inherent in its nature. Needs an even-tempered master who trains it with consistency but no harshness.
Breed character: Gentle

as a lamb when treated with affection but fierce as a lion when angered. Basically peaceful; not a great watchdog but acts as a deterrent even though it responds to strangers with reserved friendliness. Not suitable for being kept outdoors and must never be trained to become aggressive.
Problems associated with breed: None except for its size or if it doesn't get enough exercise.
Ailments associated with breed: Not much known because these dogs are quite rare. A tendency to inflammations of the mucous lining of the nose (rhinitis) has been noted.
Life expectancy: Medium.
Daily caloric needs: For a dog weighing 132 pounds (60 kg), 3,248 calories.
Remarks: This was the dog used by knights for wolf hunts or for unhorsing opponents in fights on horseback. The Irish

wolfhound is proof that a mighty, brave, and strong dog can have an entirely peaceful disposition.
Picture: In front, dark gray brindled bitch, 3½ years old; in back, cream-colored male, 3½ years old.

Irish Setter

A beautiful animal with lots of spirit. Behind this exterior is a wiry, tireless hunter: a marathon runner in a gorgeous coat.

Height, weight: 26 inches (66 cm) at the withers and a show weight of about 70 pounds (32 kg) is considered ideal for a dog (male); the bitch 25 inches (63 cm); 60 pounds (27 kg). Variance beyond an inch up or down to be discouraged. Slender, elegant, and muscular shape.

Coat and color: Thick, flat, partly short and partly longish with feathery fringe on belly, brisket, and neck. Rich chestnut-red with no trace of black; a small amount of white is permitted on chest, toes, or forehead.

Appearance: Friendly and affectionate, gives no indication of its toughness. In perfect control of its movements. The word harmonious best describes this dog.

Suitable for: People with a sense of beauty who like to spend two hours or more a day walking or riding a bicycle and who live in an average-size to large apartment.

Not suitable for: People who don't like to walk or who like to rule with an iron hand.

Requirements: The most energetic and water-loving dog in the luxury class. Needs plenty of running and affection—in this order. Not made for the big city.

Grooming: Daily brushing and ear care.

Qualities as a family member: Indifferent watchdog. Usually doesn't like riding in a car. Sheds. Affectionate, with a distinct need for physical contact, a rare trait in a proud hunting dog—which the Irish setter is even now.

Breed character: Great attachment to its master. Depending on the strain, it may be psychologically thick-skinned or oversen-

sitive. Independent and intelligent.

Problems associated with breed: Can become unpredictable and obstinate if it doesn't get enough exercise. If overbred, overly sensitive to noise and sometimes even timid.

Ailments associated with breed: Little has been reported about predisposition to specific illnesses. Watch the ears carefully to prevent ear inflammations. Ear operations for otitis often make the dogs ill-tempered afterwards.

Life expectancy: High, up to 15 years.

Daily caloric needs: For a dog weighing 44 pounds (20 kg), 1,254 calories.

Remarks: Setters have been the long-haired pointers of the British Isles for 2,000 years. There are three breeds:

The white setter has black and tan markings and is adapted to the wide fields of England (English setter).

The black setter with tan markings developed on the rocky soil of Scotland (Gordon setter, named after the Duke of Gordon). *The red setter* originated in Ireland (Irish setter). It has the most stamina and is the most versatile of the family.

Picture: Four-year-old bitch.

Shetland Sheepdog

Golden Retriever

Sometimes called a "miniature collie," this herding dog is actually a separate breed. It has become an extremely popular family dog.

A herding dog from the Shetland Islands, where sheep, too, grow small. Not a mini-collie but a breed in its own right.

Height, weight: Up to 14½ inches (36.8 cm); from 26 to 40 pounds (12–18 kg). Harmonious build.
Coat and color: Long, straight, rough top coat with wooly undercoat. Tricolored in rich tones of yellow to mahogany.
Appearance: "The most beautiful collies as seen through the wrong end of the binoculars."
Suitable for: People looking for a cheerful dog for their children.
Not suitable for: People with a lot of company.
Requirements: Easy to train. Puts up with a lot from children. Although high-spirited, it can be kept in a small apartment.
Grooming: Needs ten minutes of brushing a day.
Qualities as a family member: Adapts to the moods of its people and can be lively or sedate. Loving, and reasonable.
Breed character: Learns easily and likes to demonstrate what it has learned. Attentive and watchful; unfriendly to strangers.
Problems associated with breed: Wants to be kept busy. Loves complicated obedience exercises. Allergic to excessive discipline.
Ailments associated with breed: Not susceptible to illness; tendency to eye abnormalities.
Life expectancy: High.
Daily caloric needs: For a dog weighing 33 pounds (15 kg), 1,000 calories.
Picture: On the right, six-year-old tricolored male; on the left, eight-month-old yellow and white bitch.

With its sweet temper and its gleaming golden coat, this, the most beautiful of the retrievers, has become one of the most popular of family dogs.

Height, weight: Males up to 24½ inches (62 cm) in height at withers; females 21½ to 22½ (54½–57 cm); length from breast-bone to buttocks slightly greater than height at withers, in ratio of 12:11; up to 70 pounds (32 kg). Symmetrically built runner.
Coat and color: Smooth topcoat with dense, water-repellent undercoat. All shades of gold and cream.
Appearance: Decorative.
Suitable for: Families who have plenty of time to devote to their dog.
Not suitable for: Small apartments or people living near the woods.
Requirements: Requires a lot of exercise and things to do. Likes to perform tasks. Can be kept in the city if it is taken for walks enough.
Grooming: Easy to keep clean.
Qualities as a family member: Devoted, even-tempered, not aggressive. Gets along well with other pets. Insensitive to cold and rain. Good watchdog that doesn't bark excessively.
Breed character: Friendly, loves children, easy to walk on a leash. Likes to learn and learns easily. Loves swimming. Not aggressive.
Problems associated with breed: Needs to be kept busy. Instead of training it in hunting skills, teach it how to navigate safely in traffic.
Ailments associated with breed: With advanced age, impaired vision caused by cataracts.
Life expectancy: High.
Daily caloric needs: For a dog weighing 66 pounds (30 kg), 1,696 calories.
Picture: Six-year-old bitch with eight-week-old puppy.

Hovawart

The "dog that guards the farm" (this is the literal meaning of its name) has a long history. This is not a dog from an assembly line where each animal looks like the next but a basic type with strength and beauty; a dog that requires a strong commitment from its master.

(Recognized by the FCI)
Height, weight: Up to 27½ inches (70 cm); up to 77 pounds (35 kg). Males and females clearly different.
Coat and color: Long, slightly wavy, no undercoat, no curls, no parts in the hair. Blond, coal black, or black with blond to golden-brown markings.
Appearance: Powerful build, sturdy yet supple; impressive.
Suitable for: People who like the outdoors, are drawn to a dog that is still close to original dog nature, and who can and will assume the role of "pack leader."
Not suitable for: Beginners who want to find out what it's like to have a dog, or people who like to leave making decisions up to others.
Requirements: Needs training, work, extensive walks and outings, children or a house to guard, and a person who acts as leader and whom it accepts.
Grooming: Not much needed in spite of the long hair, because there is no shedding undercoat.
Qualities as a family member: Fits in well if guided firmly but not harshly. By nature an excellent watchdog and protector. Moves with awe-inspiring speed. Has a full, deep voice, but barks only when necessary.
Breed character: Learns well and happily; is quick to react and reliable. Courageous and tough, but can also be sensitive. Tends to be a one-person dog. The breed is recognized as a police dog. Observes a situation, thinks about it, and is ready to act quickly if necessary. Good-natured rather than ferocious.
Problems associated with breed: If overbred, it can become unreliable and be given to biting.
Ailments associated with breed: A slight tendency to hip dysplasia.
Life expectancy: Relatively high.
Daily caloric needs: A 66-pound (30 kg) dog needs 1,696 calories; a 77-pound (35 kg) animal, 1,960 calories.
Remarks: Not a new breed created by crossing existing breeds in an attempt to create a new type of dog. Instead, surviving strains of an ancient dog that used to guard farms were combined in this "reconstruction." Hovawarts have been deliberately bred again since the 1920s. The emphasis has been shifting more and more to reliable character and away from looks, which is why individual hovawarts can differ so much in appearance. There is a lightweight and a heavy type. Presence of a hovawart gives a family a sense of security.
Picture at left: Blonde bitch, four years old.
Picture at right: Two-year-old bitch with black markings.

Bernese Mountain Dog   Lhasa Apso

A picture book dog with a stunning coat in rich colors. Impressive and unmistakable.

Height, weight: Males 23 to 27½ inches (58½–70 cm); females 21 to 26 inches (53–66 cm) at the shoulders; up to 88 pounds (40 kg). Massive and strong.
Coat and color: Soft and shiny, slightly wavy. Black with deep tan markings, white blaze, feet, breast, and tip of tail.
Appearance: Inspires respect and admiration.
Suitable for: Families with children and a house with a large yard.
Not suitable for: Small apartments or people who want a dog to serve as decoration.
Requirements: Needs plenty of space and exercise. If kept outdoors, needs to be fully integrated into the family.
Grooming: Regular, thorough brushing.
Qualities as a family member: Loves children. Attentive and watchful without barking too much.
Breed character: Not exactly gentle as a lamb; but, when the situation calls for it, it can attack without immediately using its teeth on the victim. Doesn't roam or chase game. As always, it is still a herding dog.
Problems associated with breed: Slow to learn but persistent. If possible should not have to change owners after 18 months. Occasionally aggressive toward some family members.
Ailments associated with breed: Hip dysplasia.
Life expectancy: Medium.
Daily caloric needs: A dog weighing 77 pounds (35 kg), 1,960 calories.
Remarks: Willing to work, also for trials. The dog first entered the United States and was given recognition in the middle 1930s.
Picture: Five-year-old male.

A cheerful, affectionate Tibetan dog that has become extremely popular in the West.

Height, weight: 9½ to 11 inches (24–28 cm); 11 to 15 pounds (5–7 kg). Rectangular silhouette.
Coat and color: Heavy, dense, and abundant coat in two layers. The hair hangs down straight. The tail is carried over the back but hidden under the hair. Many different colors: there are no two identical Apsos.
Appearance: Unusual.
Suitable for: People who like something different.
Not suitable for: People with an aversion to hair.
Requirements: Needs close contact with its family. An apartment dog.
Grooming: Coat needs to be groomed regularly and intensively every day. None of the fur gets trimmed.
Qualities as a family member: Has a mind of its own but is watchful and intelligent. Likes to show off. Its cheerfulness is infectious.
Breed character: Affectionate with its own people but unfriendly with strangers.
Problems associated with breed: Has a voice that carries far and that it likes to use.
Ailments associated with breed: Not susceptible to illness and very hardy.
Life expectancy: High; 15 years and more.
Daily caloric needs: 600 calories.
Picture: On the right, two-year-old red gold bitch; on the left, one-year-old light gold bitch.
Remarks: Since the Chinese occupation of its Tibetan homeland, this breed has died out there. The breed has retained its abundant hair and lovable character.

Newfoundland

A huge dog with a massive head and gentle eyes. A coal black giant that moves with surprising grace. The best swimmer among dogs.

Height, weight: Males up to 28 inches (71 cm); females 26 inches (66 cm); weight according to size, from 110 to 137 pounds (50–62 kg). Powerful, impressive figure.

Coat and color: Long, dense, and smooth. Hard, coarse, and oily to the touch. Black, black with a tinge of brown. Brown possible but rare. A larger black and white variety was established in 1960 as a separate breed, named Landseer.

Appearance: The dominant impression of this dog derives from its thick fur. Has webs between its toes.

Suitable for: Families with children, lots of room, and a lake nearby, or people who spend a lot of time on and near water.

Not suitable for: The big city or small apartments.

Requirements: Apart from its enjoyment of water this dog doesn't make great demands. Hates the heat.

Grooming: Must be curried regularly; should not be bathed.

Qualities as a family member: Good-tempered; gets along with cats and other pets. Marked desire to protect the weak against stronger aggressors. This makes it an ideal companion for children. Needs an even-tempered master to whom it subordinates itself unquestioningly. Moves with caution indoors. Can be kept outdoors if there is enough contact with the family.

Breed character: Peaceful, not a bully. Good watchdog that barks little—its growl is enough to frighten intruders away. Very attached to its people and cannot bear having to leave them for a new home. Lord Byron wrote of it that it "possessed...all the Virtues of Man, without his Vices."

Problems associated with breed: If it spends a lot of time in the water, it smells "doggy."

Ailments associated with breed: Tendency to develop hip dysplasia; narrowing of the aorta (aortic stenosis).

Life expectancy: Medium.

Daily caloric needs: For a dog weighing 121 pounds (55 kg), 2,990 calories.

Remarks: The Newfoundland dogs that used to help the fishermen of Newfoundland pull fishnets to shore and gather the fish that had slipped through the net didn't necessarily look like the giant Newfoundland of today. They were more like sled dogs and pulled loads on land as well. The first breed club for Newfoundlands was founded in 1886 in England. It is relatively easy to train Newfoundlands for water rescue work. (They grab a drowning person by the arm, then pull the victim to shore.)

Picture: Five-year-old black male.

Kuvasz

Rottweiler

The name is Turkish and means "security guard." This beautiful dog is of Hungarian nationality.

Height, weight: Males up to 30 inches (75 cm); females, 26 to 28 inches (66–71 cm); up to 88 pounds (40 kg). Large and well-proportioned.
Coat and color: Coarse and wavy. Some feathering on tail. Pure white; may also be ivory.
Appearance: Majestic, strong, and commanding respect.
Suitable for: People who know dogs and want an incorruptible watchdog.
Not suitable for: Beginners who dream of a big, strong dog.
Requirements: Not an apartment dog. Can be kept outdoors if it stays in close contact with its family.
Grooming: Must be curried and brushed regularly.
Qualities as a family member: Lively temperament. Very affectionate toward the children of its family but suspicious of other children. Affectionate but not cuddly. Can't bear unjust treatment.
Breed character: Very brave; good watchdog; famous for its intelligence. Doesn't subordinate itself easily and therefore cannot be trained as a police dog.
Problems associated with breed: Needs close human contact or will revert to wildness and become dangerous.
Ailments associated with breed: Susceptible to distemper.
Life expectancy: About ten years.
Daily caloric needs: For an 88-pound (40 kg) dog, 2,100 calories.
Remarks: Capable of trotting as much as 15½ miles (25 km) at a stretch and needs lots of exercise.
Picture: Three-year-old male.

This butcher's dog from Württemberg is named after the town of Rottweil. A beautiful and powerful dog with a stump of a tail.

Height, weight: Males up to 27 inches (68 cm); bitches up to 25¾ inches (65.5 cm); about 110 pounds (50 kg).
Coat and color: Coarse, short, flat topcoat with good undercoat. Coal black with clearly defined mahogany markings.
Appearance: Imposing and menacing rather than friendly.
Suitable for: Sports-loving families with children and a yard.
Not suitable for: Sedentary people or anyone lacking experience with dogs.
Requirements: Needs plenty of exercise and work, if possible together with other dogs.
Grooming: Not much needed.
Qualities as a family member: Sturdy and uncomplicated. Good watchdog without barking much. Excellent family dog. A run in the yard is best for it, but there has to be close contact with the family.
Breed character: Slow to develop physically and mentally. Good learning ability. Fearless, persevering, and robust. Reliable temperament; doesn't roam.
Problems associated with breed: These are strong fighters that seem immune to pain and are not very popular on dog training fields.
Ailments associated with breed: Entropion (narrowing of the slit between the eyelids); hip dysplasia has been practically eliminated. Robust health.
Life expectancy: About ten years.
Daily caloric needs: For a dog weighing 110 pounds (50 kg), 2,720 calories.
Picture: Six-year-old male.

Labrador Retriever

The Labrador retriever was originally a hunting dog specializing in waterfowl. It is emotionally stable, easy to guide, and is now appreciated primarily as a companion dog rather than a hunter.

Height, weight: 21½ to 24½ inches (55–62 cm); bitches 21½ to 23½ inches (54.5–60 cm); 55 to 68 pounds (25–31 kg). Strong and blocky.
Coat and color: Short, hard, without wave or feathering on legs and tail. Water-repellent undercoat. The tail is covered all around with thick fur (otter tail). Black or yellow, of uniform color and without spots.
Appearance: Friendly. Suggesting effortless action and quick movement.
Suitable for: Families with children, people who like walking and are willing to spend a lot of time with their dog. Can be used for hunting.

Not suitable for: Small apartments, indoor people, city people, or people with very little time.
Requirements: Adjusts beautifully to all kinds of situations, whether it be at home, traveling, in the thick of traffic, or in the countryside.
Grooming: Regular brushing; otherwise requires little care.
Qualities as a family member: Very fond of children, friendly, and easy to train. Doesn't pull on the leash. Gets along with other dogs and pets. Relatively good watch-dog. Very devoted to its people; should not be kept outdoors.
Breed character: Basically peaceful; not noisy; very reliable, even in city traffic. Courageous and persistent.
Problems associated with breed: Since this is a very active dog that likes to work—it was originally a hardy hunting dog—it should not be

pampered or left without occupation. It especially loves retrieving things during walks.
Ailments associated with breed: Hip dysplasia and, in some breed families, hemophilia. On the whole robust and healthy.
Life expectancy: High.
Daily caloric needs: For a dog weighing 55 pounds (25 kg), 1,480 calories; for a 66–pound (30 kg) dog, 1,700 calories. On a day out hunting, a dog needs considerably more calories.
Remarks: Retrievers are still used extensively for hunting. There are several different retrievers: The *curly-coated retriever*, the *flat-coated retriever*, the *Chesapeake Bay retriever*, the *Nova Scotia duck tolling retriever*, the *Labrador retriever*, and the *golden retriever*. The last two have been getting more and more popular as companion dogs. Labrador and golden retrievers also are very

good at detecting narcotics and are used as Seeing Eye dogs as well.
Picture: Yellow male, six years old.

German Spitz
Wolfspitz, giant, standard, miniature, and toy spitz

The spitz with its gorgeous coat comes in five varieties that differ only in size. A breed that deserves again the widespread popularity it once enjoyed.

(Recognized by the FCI)
Height,weight: Wolfspitz: 21½ inches (55 cm); 55 to 62 pounds (25–28 kg). Giant: 16 to 20 inches (40–50 cm); 55 pounds (25 kg). Standard: 12½ inches (32 cm); 13 to 15 pounds (6–7 kg). Miniature: 9 to 11 inches (23–28 cm); 9 to 11 pounds (4–5 kg). Toy: up to 8½ inches (22 cm); 4½ to 6½ pounds (2–3 kg). Straight body with a short back.
Coat and color: Fluffy, sticking out from the body and forming a mane. Neither wavy nor shaggy. Colors, depending on type, from wolf gray and silver to black, white, brown, and orange; also blue and cream.
Appearance: Foxy head

and lots of fur. Closely resembles the keeshond.
Suitable for: People who don't mind dog hair and have no noise-sensitive neighbors.
Not suitable for: People with noise-sensitive neighbors, expensive carpets and fancy upholstered furniture; anyone who likes to wear neat-looking, dark clothes.
Requirements: Depending on the size of the dog, anything from a small apartment to a house with a yard that the dog can guard. Needs things to do and is always eager to learn.
Grooming: Careful daily brushing with a brush of natural bristles. Always work from the back to the front.
Qualities as a family member: The smaller the dog, the more it barks. Suspicious of strangers, good watchdog. Stays close to home and doesn't roam or chase game.
Breed character: Great intelligence and eager-

ness to learn, easy to guide. Affectionate and faithful. Pleasant and loving with its family. The giant spitz is a reliable companion dog, the miniature spitz does well in the city, and the toy spitz is a lap dog.
Problems associated with breed: The constant yapping is more a neurotic habit than a feature of the breed. It is possible to reduce the barking through training.
Ailments associated with breed: Generally healthy and robust. Toy spitzes are subject to kidney stones, dislocated kneecaps, and bronchitis brought on by old age.
Life expectancy: The spitz group are the most long-lived dogs.
Daily caloric needs: Wolfsspitz and giant spitz: about 1,480 calories. Standard spitz: 575 calories. Miniature and toy spitzes: about 260 calories.
Remarks: There is an old German saying that is still

basically true: "As long as a spitz barks near the door, the farm is safe." This is an ancient German breed, and the names of some strains indicate where those strains originated: The Mannheim spitz is a black miniature spitz, and the Weinberg spitz, a black giant spitz from Swabia. The spitz is not a fashionable dog, and after a revival of interest in the 1970s, its numbers are again on the decline.
Picture, left: Toy spitzes; on the left, wolf-colored female, 1½ years old; on the right, orange male, eight months old.
Picture, right: Wolfspitz bitch, light gray with dark gray, two years old.

Airedale Terrier

Dalmatian

This "king of terriers" is a courageous dog that was in earlier days used to hunt otters on land and in the water.

Height, weight: 23 to 24 inches (58–61 cm); 50 pounds (22.5 kg). Well-proportioned and agile.
Coat and color: Double coat; dense, wiry topcoat with short, soft undercoat. Tan with black or dark grizzle on saddle.
Appearance: Wiry and expressive.
Suitable for: People who want an uncomplicated dog that can also protect them.
Not suitable for: Frail or very fussy people.
Requirements: Needs a large apartment, if possible with access to a yard; also lots of running.
Grooming: Has to be clipped every 8 to 12 weeks.
Qualities as a family member: Excellent family dog, fond of children. Good watchdog. Good-

natured, hardly ever gets angry.
Breed character: Intelligent; good learner; likes to be kept busy. Adjusts where adjustment is necessary. Lively and playful into old age.
Problems associated with breed: Hard to keep together with other dogs or pets.
Ailments associated with breed: Tends to develop eczema and skin swellings.
Life expectancy: High.
Daily caloric needs: For a dog weighing 44 pounds (20 kg), 1,250 calories.
Remarks: This is a recognized working breed and can therefore be trained for trials in the utility class.
Picture: Three-year-old male.

A cheerful long-distance runner that looks conspicuous because of the dark spots splashed on its white coat.

Height, weight: 20 to 23 inches (50–58 cm); any dog or bitch over 24 inches (61 cm) at the withers is to be disquali-fied; up to 55 pounds (25 kg). Well proportioned and muscular.
Coat and color: Short, hard, dense, sleek, and glossy. Pure white with small, clearly defined, and well-distributed spots, either black or liver.
Appearance: Eccentric.
Suitable for: Sports-oriented families with children.
Not suitable for: People who like a placid dog or who don't like to draw attention to themselves.
Requirements: Large apartment, large yard, plenty of exercise.
Grooming: Not much needed, but likes to be kept clean.

Qualities as a family member: Watchful, not given to biting, not noisy. Doesn't like to "lose scent" of its master.
Breed character: Uncomplicated and cheerful; therefore easy to teach. Adaptable and docile. Loves running.
Problems associated with breed: Needs an even-tempered master, because it reflects its master's moods.
Ailments associated with breed: On the whole not susceptible to disease. Sometimes eczema or kidney stones resulting from a buildup of uric acid.
Life expectancy: High.
Daily caloric needs: For a dog weighing 55 pounds (25 kg), 1,480 calories.
Remarks: Used to accompany horseback riders and stagecoaches in earlier times; also known as a firehouse dog from running with fire trucks.
Picture: Six-year-old male.

Schnauzer
Miniature, standard, and giant schnauzer

Solid dogs in three sizes with bushy eyebrows and beards. In the old days they accompanied delivery wagons and kept the cities free of rats. The giant schnauzer originated in upper Bavaria.

Height, weight: Miniature: 12 to 14 inches (30–35 cm); 18 pounds (8 kg). Standard: 18 to 20 inches (45–50 cm); 33 to 40 pounds (15–18 kg). Giant: 24 to 28 inches (60–70 cm); about 88 pounds (40 kg). Heavyset rather than slender—in all sizes.

Coat and color: Hard, rough-haired, and thick; typically has a wiry beard. Pure black or pepper and salt. Toy schnauzers also black and silver with white markings.

Appearance: Trim, energetic, able to defend itself; not necessarily friendly.

Suitable for: People who are more interested in substance than appear-ance. Can be kept in a small or larger apartment or in a house with yard (also with children).

Not suitable for: Indecisive or soft-hearted people.

Requirements: Depending on the size of the dog, an apartment or house. All schnauzers need lots of exercise, and giant schnauzers need to be kept busy.

Grooming: Regular trimming and clipping.

Qualities as a family member: Excellent watchdog. Marked sense of property which, in the toy schnauzer, expresses itself in barking. Suspicious of strangers. Playful into old age.

Breed character: Psychologically sensitive (despite physical robustness). Easy to moderately difficult to train. Suspicious toward strangers; courageous even in toy size.

Problems associated with breed: Giant schnauzers have to have enough to do, or they may become troublesome (accumulation of aggression). Training has to be executed very rigorously since these dogs mature slowly and are very playful. Toy schnauzers like to assume the role of family tyrant.

Ailments associated with breed: Not susceptible to disease. In some breed families, a tendency to develop kidney stones. In toys, degeneration of hip joint (not hip dysplasia) when still young.

Life expectancy: High; in toys, very high.

Daily caloric needs: Toy: 640 calories. Standard: for a 33–pound (15 kg) dog, 1,000 calories. Giant: 2,100 calories.

Remarks: Schnauzers are related to the pinschers. Considering the breed's great age (its German name "Rattler" has been around for centuries), the name "schnauzer" is relatively recent, having become the official breed name only after World War I. The giant schnauzer works as a police, customs, and Seeing Eye dog and is also used to sniff out narcotics and explosives. All three sizes are similar in looks. The toy breed (a miniature replica of its larger relatives) lacks all the flaws associated with toy dogs. It can be taken along anywhere and is an ideal dog for the big city.

Picture, left: Male toy schnauzer, black and silver, 1½ years old.

Picture, right: Standard schnauzer bitch, pepper and salt, 6 years old.

Picture on page 60: Black giant schnauzer.

Poodle
Toy poodle, miniature poodle, standard poodle

A lovable dog that comes in three sizes. The writer Peter Scheitlein said of it a century ago: "The poodle is the most perfect dog. It has individuality, distinctiveness, originality, and geniality. It is all psyche."

Height, weight: Miniature (original strain): 14 to 18 inches (35–45 cm); about 33 pounds (15 kg). Standard: 18 to 23 inches (45–58 cm); up to 49 pounds (22 kg). Toy: 11 to 14 inches (28–35 cm); about 9 pounds (4 kg). Square build of harmonious proportions.
Coat and colors: Profuse, wooly, harsh, and curly hair clipped to characteristic shape. Black, white, gray, brown, solid silver, and apricot.
Appearance: A lively and alert dog with a light, dancing gait, it gives the impression of pride, elegance, and intelligence.
Suitable for: People

living alone or families with children—anyone living in the city and wanting a dog that learns easily. There is a right size for anyone.
Not suitable for: Overbearing, impatient, or nervous types.
Requirements: The space needs vary from a tiny to a large apartment, depending on the size of the breed. Standard poodles appreciate a yard. If a poodle is given enough opportunity to run and play, it can adjust to all kinds of living conditions, but it cannot bear loneliness.
Grooming: A thorough brushing and combing three times a week. Frequency of visits to the dog parlor depend on the style of clipping.
Qualities as a family member: No great interest in other dogs; concentrates all its attention on its family and tries to perform what it has learned over and over before an audience. This

can be tiresome; in any case, a poodle requires almost constant attention. Good watchdog, which, in the case of a standard poodle, is an effective quality. Toy poodles can be yappy. Poodles don't shed.
Breed character: Sociable and charming. Very affectionate; enjoys physical contact and is eager to learn. Always alert and ready for anything. The writer Richard Katz has summed up the nature of this breed: "The essence of a poodle is part clown, part angel, and part devil. But the proportions vary greatly from dog to dog." Poodles are not only easy to train, they also learn tricks easily.
Problems associated with breed: A poodle likes to be the center of attention, which can become a nuisance, especially if the dog is too excitable (which is the case rather frequently with toys). If such a dog is

spoiled or treated as a surrogate child, it can become hysterical. Neurotic dogs of this sort yap constantly, are excessively jealous of their people, and rule like tyrants over their owners or the entire family. All poodles need to have their ears checked frequently, and precautions should be taken against buildup of tartar on the teeth.
Ailments associated with breed: Brown poodles tend to become prematurely gray. The following tendencies are common especially in toy poodles: nervous licking of the paws and pulling out of hair; tonsillitis; herniated disks; epileptic attacks; kidney stones; and, in case of young dogs, dislocated kneecaps. This loosening of the knee joint is quite common in toy poodles and is usually congenital.
Life expectancy: All varieties can live to 12 years and more.

Daily caloric needs:
Miniature: 1,000 calories.
Standard poodle weighing
44 pounds (20 kg): 1,250
calories. Toy: 395
calories.

Note on clipping: If you
plan to enter your poodle
in a show, it has to be
clipped to one of the
standard patterns:

Continental clip, in which
the face, hindquarters,
and front legs are shorn.
Bracelets are left on the
front and back feet, a
pom-pom on the tip of the
tail, and a mane or jacket
extending from the head
to the chest and across
the ribs.

Puppy clip, in which fur is
left on the front and hind
legs, a pom-pom on the
tail, and the hair is left
long on the top of the
head and the ears (see
photo above). This is the
more common style. At
shows, of two dogs that
are otherwise equal in
quality, the one in
continental clip is to be
given preference over the
one in puppy clip.

Corded poodles, whose
fine, wooly hair forms
strings, or cords, at least
eight inches (20 cm) long
are accepted at shows,
but they are not in fashion
at present. Corded
poodles require a great
deal of grooming and
experience.

Remarks: Poodle-like
dogs are depicted in art
as early as the thirteenth
century, and later artists
like Rembrandt and Goya
painted poodles. In his
Natural History of Animals
(1749), George de Buffon
describes two sizes of
poodles and the continen-
tal clip. This style of
clipping reflected not only
esthetic tastes but also
practical requirements;
the poodle was not just a
lap dog but was also used
for hunting in the water.
The continental clip made
swimming easier and
allowed the dog to dry
faster afterwards.
The "poodle boom" at the
end of the eighteenth
century, when everybody
in high society had a

poodle and drawing
rooms were decorated
with silver or porcelain
poodle figurines, had a
revival almost 200 years
later. In the 1960s
poodles were the
fashionable breed par
excellence. Many people
who couldn't own one in
the flesh had at least a
replica in ceramics or in
the pattern on a scarf or
umbrella. There were
poodles everywhere.
Some people changed the
tint of their poodle's hair
every four weeks to match
their own, and breeders
introduced new colors like
blue-gray, cafe au lait,
and bicolors to meet the
competition of synthetic
colors. There was even an
extremely popular hair
style for women that was
known as the "poodle cut."
Today, the poodle
remains one of the most
popular dogs worldwide,
but for the time being the
poodle fad is over.
Picture on page 148,
left: Apricot toy poodle
bitch, four years old.

Picture on page 148,
left: Apricot toy poodle
bitch;
right: Black miniature
poodle bitch.
Picture, above: White
standard poodle bitch,
three years old.

Cocker Spaniel
and other spaniels

"The dog with the eyes that never lie" is a hard-working, strong hunting dog that has turned into a companion and family dog. The English spaniel is the most common spaniel type.

Height, weight: Males up to 15 inches (38 cm); bitches up to 14 inches (35½ cm); height may vary ½ inch (1 cm) above or below this ideal; 27½ to 32 pounds (12.5–14.5 kg). American cockers somewhat smaller—14 to 15 inches (35.5–38.1 cm) —and lighter. Cocker Spaniels are of compact build.

Coat and color: Smooth and silky, not wavy. Not excessively feathered. Solid black or red, black with red markings, black and white, orange and white, black and white with tan, red roan, orange roan (see pictures above, right, and on page 151), brown-roan with tan, and blue-roan. American cocker spaniels have thicker fur, especially on the ears, and the hair is less wavy. Marked eyebrows. Colors the same as for English cockers.

Appearance: A decidedly pretty dog that moves with elegance. Its body measures the same from the ground to the withers as from the withers to the base of the tail. American cockers have rounder heads.

Suitable for: People who like sensitive, affectionate dogs and who have plenty of time for grooming and long walks. Also people who are not too fussy about their possessions.

Not suitable for: People who don't know the difference between authority and harshness and people who have light-colored upholstery that they want to stay clean.

Requirements: Needs more exercise than one might think—a long walk every day. Also ear checks and coat care are very time-consuming. Be consistent in not overfeeding.

Grooming: Daily combing and brushing; use a special comb for cocker spaniels. Occasional plucking and trimming with hair-thinning scissors. Regular ear checks at home and every so often by the veterinarian.

Qualities as a family member: Not a reliable watchdog. Drools if at all excited and is therefore not popular with everybody. Barks more outdoors than in. Makes the most of any weakness in its owner and therefore requires firm training.

Breed character: Ranges from playful and exuberant to loving, affectionate, and sensitive. Still by nature a tireless hunter. Spaniels are easy to train and guide.

Problems associated with breed: Cocker spaniels are real gluttons and beg with charm and an irresistible expression.

Keep the calories down and check the weight frequently. Some scientists suspect that the gene for the color red is associated with a gene that causes aggressiveness. Other scientists ascribe occasional incidents of "cocker madness" to wrong treatment on the part of the owner. Fully grown red male cockers are subject to such attacks, during which they bite without warning or provocation. There is no treatment.

Ailments associated with breed: Ear infections, eczema in the fold of the lower lip, dislocated knee cap, congenital glaucoma, and a tendency to melanoma and to lumps caused by plugged sebaceous glands.

Life expectancy: Up to 16 years.

Daily caloric needs: For a dog weighing 29 pounds (13 kg), 975 calories.

Cavalier King Charles Spaniel

Remarks about the spaniel family: Spaniels, if they are not used for hunting, need at least a one-hour walk daily with a longer jaunt once a week. Because of their hunting background, letting them run loose is impractical, and the use of a leash with an automatic roll-up mechanism is therefore a good solution because it gives a dog about 15 feet (5 m) of leeway.

The *Welsh springer* is white and dark rich red. It is excellent at finding and retrieving birds.

The *English springer* works particularly well in thick brush.

The *Irish water spaniel* with its curly coat is especially well adapted to work in water.

The *clumber spaniel* is powerful and heavy and used for hunting pheasants.

The *field spaniel* is used for hunting on open ground.

The *Sussex spaniel* barks while following a scent.

Picture on page 150, left: Orange-roan male, five years old, with ten-week-old puppy.

Picture on page 150, right: three cocker spaniels; from left to right: Orange-roan male, five years old; four-year-old bitch, brown-roan with tan; four-year-old male, blue roan.

Picture on page 151, left: Two-year-old bitch, brown-roan with tan.

A graceful small spaniel with expressive eyes, a noticeable stop, and a short muzzle.

Height, weight: Up to 12 inches (30 cm); 9 to 18 pounds (4–8 kg). Elegant and strong.

Coat and color: Long, silky, and without curls; slightly wavy hair permitted. Black and white with tan markings. Also bright chestnut-red on pearly white (Blenheim), black and chestnut or ruby-red (Ruby), or black and tan.

Appearance: Very elegant, with the motions of a spaniel.

Suitable for: People who would like to have a normal spaniel but in a more compact size.

Not suitable for: People who want a true luxury dog (to grace their couch).

Requirements: Adjusts to all kinds of situations. If there is enough room, it is preferable to keep two or three of these dogs.

Grooming: Daily brushing and combing.

Qualities as a family member: Easy to train; loves long walks, yet can be kept in a small apartment. Cheerful and lively, very friendly.

Breed character: Reliable temperament, fond of children (which is not all that common in small breeds), and gets along well with other dogs. Good hunter.

Problems associated with breed: Requires regular checking of the ears and attention if the eyes tear.

Ailments associated with breed: Congenital abnormality of the eyelids (distichiasis); namely, eyelashes growing in the wrong place. Dislocation of the kneecap. But on the whole of robust health.

Life expectancy: High.

Daily caloric needs: For a 15-pound (7 kg) dog, 590 calories.

Picture: Black and tan male, five years old.

Akita

Siberian Husky

The Akita is Japanese in origin and is the most imposing representative of the international spitz family.

Height, weight: 26 to 28 inches (66–71 cm); bitches 24 to 26 inches (61–66 cm); males under 25 inches (63.5 cm) and bitches under 23 inches (58 cm) will be disqualified; up to 106 pounds (48 kg). Solid and substantial.
Coat and color: Stiff outer coat with dense, soft undercoat. All colors permitted; commonly red with a lighter mask or chestnut with darker mask.
Appearance: Robust and rather menacing. The ringtail carried high is typical.
Suitable for: People who know something about dogs, who are willing to deal with the Akita's strong will, and who are looking for an unusual dog.
Not suitable for: People who appreciate subordination in a dog or who live in a neighborhood with lots of dogs.
Requirements: Takes a lot of love and patience. Likes to work and be occupied.
Grooming: Not much needed.
Qualities as a family member: Affectionate and obedient toward its family. Quiet, even-tempered, courageous. Rather indifferent toward strangers. Watchful.
Breed character: Cannot be forced to do anything.
Problems associated with breed: Can be very strong-willed.
Ailments associated with breed: Hip dysplasia, faulty dentition.
Life expectancy: Not described.
Daily caloric needs: For a dog weighing 100 pounds (45 kg), 2,260 calories.
Picture: 7½-month-old male, red with light mask.

The world's most popular sled dog is only for specialists. It is very tough and strong.

Height, weight: Up to 23 inches (59 cm); up to 60 pounds (27 kg). Fast and light-footed.
Coat and color: Topcoat made up of straight, medium-long, and smooth guard hairs; soft undercoat. From pure white to black; most often black and white with gray.
Appearance: A wolf with brown or blue eyes or one eye of each color.
Suitable for: Enthusiastic participants in winter sports who like to drive sleds and training carts.
Not suitable for: People who like to stay home and are physically inactive.
Requirements: Needs relatively little room but much freedom of movement outdoors. Wants to pull and preferably live in packs.
Grooming: Has to be combed thoroughly with a metal comb during shedding season.
Qualities as a family member: Not aggressive toward humans. Pleasant, open, but has a will of its own. Needs a human leader to follow.
Breed character: Its need for running and urge for independence are so great that the husky does not make a good companion dog. If they live together in a pack, huskies interact constantly, thus using up their excess energies.
Problems associated with breed: If huskies are not allowed to pull, they begin to roam, which can be dangerous.
Ailments associated with breed: A robust dog. Has a tendency to develop ectopy (displacement) of the urethra.
Life expectancy: Not described.
Daily caloric needs: For a 55-pound (25 kg) dog, 1,480 calories.
Picture: Gray and white bitch, seven years old.

Beagle

A cheerful hunting dog that works in packs and goes after hares, it is both gentle and obstinate. It has a sturdy body with elegant contours. Being of a "handy" size, it has become a good indoor and family dog.

Height, weight: Not less than 13 nor more than 16 inches (33–41 cm); between 22 and 40 pounds (10–18 kg). Jollity is a major trait of the breed.

Coat and color: Short, dense, and hard; the tail is thick and covered with thick hair, always with a white tip. All true hound colors, never chocolate brown. Most commonly tricolored—black and brown to reddish patches on white ground—or bicolored, as tan and white or lemon and white.

Appearance: Gentle expression on the smooth face that is dominated by the nose. The looks of the beagle show that it tracks

game by scent.

Suitable for: Physically active people who want a lively, apartment-size dog that likes children.

Not suitable for: People who consider toughness an essential quality in a dog.

Requirements: Needs human company and becomes attached to the whole family (the pack) rather than one individual. Regular walks, if possible running along beside a bicycle; always on a long leash.

Grooming: Not much needed (rub the dog's coat down wearing gloves with rubber nubbles).

Qualities as a family member: Pleasant; barks very little; very sociable and friendly. Not an especially good watchdog. Its sociability is so strong that it greets any visitor with a wagging tail; a thief—once inside—would be regarded as welcome company. Likes to play and generally makes a good playmate

for children.

Breed character: Sociable (likes sharing the household with other dogs), adaptable, and affectionate. Reliable temperament; shouldn't be allowed to become sharp and aggressive. Likes to avoid having to obey commands. Self-assured and independent.

Problems associated with breed: Even when given plenty of exercise, beagles like to take off in pursuit of scents once they break out of their master's sphere of authority. Not altogether easy to train, because the beagle is full of self-confidence in spite of its polite manners. The most common cause of death is being run over by cars.

Ailments associated with breed: Robust dog. Little is known about special susceptibilities. The preferred breed for animal experiments.

Life expectancy: 12 years.

Daily caloric needs: For

a dog weighing 33 pounds (15 kg), 1,000 calories.

Remarks: The traditional dog for hunting hares, either in dog packs or singly. Following a scent is often required of them, too. For hunting on horseback, packs of beagles are used primarily.

Picture: On left, tricolor bitch, six years old; on right: ten year-old bitch, mottled tricolor.

Bullterrier

Not everybody finds this muscular dog with its ram's nose and noncommittal facial expression attractive. In character it has changed from a "gladiator" to an "aristocrat."

Height, weight: About 21 inches (54 cm); maximum weight around 50 to 62 pounds (23–28 kg). Should not be fat but smooth and muscular.

Coat and color: Short, flat, and glossy; hard to the touch. Pure white with markings on head (monocles); brindle or red, tan or tricolor.

Appearance: A bundle of energy. People who don't know much about dogs sometimes compare white bullterriers with their visibly pink skin to piglets.

Suitable for: People who know how to handle dogs or families with some room—not necessarily very much—and somebody who is willing to devote time to the dog.

Not suitable for: The average person or people with conventional notions of beauty.

Requirements: Needs lots of love, which it amply rewards; enough space for exercise; a very high garden fence or an outdoor run where it can spend a couple of hours at a time. But can also be kept with only limited space available. Needs patient and firm training.

Grooming: Not much needed.

Qualities as a family member: Reliable watchdog and protector. Not excessively noisy. Loves to play with children. Becomes a true member of the family and adores its people.

Breed character: Self-willed to the point of obstinacy, but easily guided by an experienced handler and unreservedly devoted to its master. Doesn't pick fights but is unbeatable if attacked. Doesn't seem to feel pain. Can tell the strong from

the weak and the big from the small. Enjoys hours of walking but will just as happily lie around idly.

Problems associated with breed: Can be jealous. Totally unconscious of the dangers of big-city traffic. Litter mates of the same sex hardly ever get along together. If not properly trained or if taught to be aggressive, the bullterrier can be truly dangerous.

Ailments associated with breed: Sensitive to the wet and the cold (kidney problems). Deafness in white animals. Constriction of the heart valves.

Life expectancy: High, about 14 years.

Daily caloric needs: For a dog weighing 55 pounds (25 kg), 1,480 calories.

Remarks: In the nineteenth century this dog was bred exclusively to fight bulls and other bullterriers. The breed distinguished itself by its strength, agility, and courage. This heritage

fascinates some people today who see in the dog a "weapon" that requires no permit. This is one reason that the bullterrier, which has since its fighting days developed into a friendly dog, should be kept only by people of solid character.

Picture, left: On the left, five-year-old bitch, red with white; on the right, four-year-old gold brindle with markings.

Picture, right: One-year-old male, white with black markings.

Fox terrier
Smooth and wirehaired

A whirlwind of a dog, built like a good hunting horse. Always ready to go, combative, elegant, daring, enterprising. Highly intelligent and a true comrade for adventures.

Height, weight: Not over 15½ inches (39.4 cm); about 18 pounds (8 kg). Always looks ready to spring into action.
Coat and color: Smooth: hard, dense, and abundant; predominantly white with brown or black patches and markings on the head. Wire-haired: curly and close; should be as dense and wiry as a coconut-fiber mat. One should not be able to part the hair down to the skin. The undercoat is soft. Colors same as in smooth strain.
Appearance: Alert, attentive, full of cunning cleverness, and filled with boundless energy.
Suitable for: Cheerful people—including families with children—who are not easily upset.
Not suitable for: Fearful, insecure, and nervous people who have trouble asserting themselves.
Requirements: Needs more space than its size would suggest and should live in an apartment of at least moderate size, if possible with access to a yard. Should have regular structured activities; games; and long walks, preferably on a leash.
Grooming: Not much needed for the smooth strain. The wirehaired fox terrier needs to be shaped four times a year with shearing scissors, hair scissors, a trimming knife, and plucking. If you don't have a gift for "sculpting" a dog, take your wirehair to a beauty specialist.
Qualities as a family member: Good watchdog that does its job with great zeal and sometimes an excess of noise. Never tires of children. Travels well in a car and protects the car.

Breed character: Intelligent; tends to exploit its owner's weaknesses. Reliable temperament, bold, active, but not restless. Can sit motionless for hours in front of a rat hole. Painstaking and firm training strongly recommended. A cheerful dog that will bring laughter into your life.
Problems associated with breed: Tends to get jealous if neglected. Sometimes likes to pick fights. Dogs from some kennels are high-strung. Hard to keep together with other dogs, even other fox terriers.
Ailments associated with breed: May develop kidney stones, glaucoma, and, in later years, diabetes. Most visits to the veterinarian are to treat wounds sustained in fights.
Life expectancy: 12 to 14 years.
Daily caloric needs: For a dog weighing 16 pounds (7.5 kg), 600 calories.
Remarks: Fox terriers were used in the early nineteenth century for fox hunts on horseback. In the 1920s and 1930s, the wirehaired fox terrier became highly fashionable, with questionable results for the breed, when thousands of litters were registered in a single year. When the fox terrier's popularity began to wane, the breed recovered in quality. The smooth strain is considerably rarer than its wirehaired cousin.
Picture: On the left, 2½-year-old wirehaired bitch, white with brown and black markings. On the right, two-year-old smooth-haired male, brown and white.

English Bulldog

This old English fighting dog has become one of the most loving family dogs. It is unmistakable with its powerful skull and compact, broad body.

Height, weight: No prescribed height; around 16 inches (40 cm); ideal weight: 53 pounds (24 kg). Good-natured powerhouse.

Coat and color: Thick, short, and fine-textured. White, reddish, reddish yellow, fawn, or brindle. The purity of color is more important than the shade. Only black is considered undesirable even in spots.

Appearance: Somewhere between grotesque and sullenly intimidating. Not a dog everybody is wild about.

Suitable for: Families with children who like to display unusual taste. Individualists who accept that even a dog should be allowed to have its own personality.

Not suitable for: People active in sports or anyone who wants a dog that obeys perfectly.

Requirements: Isn't overly fond of long walks. Not as heat-sensitive as many people say. Needs love, which it repays many times over. Can be kept even in a small apartment.

Grooming: Not much needed except for regular and careful cleaning of the skin folds.

Qualities as a family member: Good-natured, patient, hardly ever excitable; incorruptible. Has a high threshold of tolerance, and it takes a great deal to make this dog angry. Once it bites, however, (bulldogs defend their family with great vigor) it doesn't let go.

Breed character: The ideal bulldog is active and has an elegance of propulsion characteristic of some heavy creatures. This dog is not supposed to be aggressive. It is so set in its ways that even very firm training has little effect. The dog's personality is so strong that most owners fall under its spell and become devoted bulldog fans. Bulldogs are more interested in their people than in other dogs.

Problems associated with breed: Wheezes audibly as it breathes. Its digestive system is very active and may be offensive to people with sensitive noses. Keep the skin folds clean.

Ailments associated with breed: Breathing difficulties and reluctance to mate. Because of puppies' broad heads, Caesarean delivery is often necessary. On the whole, however, a robust dog without physical complaints.

Life expectancy: Medium.

Daily caloric needs: For a dog weighing 53 pounds (24 kg), 1,430 calories.

Remarks: Famed and notorious fighters of bulls, bears, and badgers. Some dogs were as famous in their heyday as football stars are today. The national dog of England, it symbolizes the English virtues of courage, persistence, and composure. Formerly, in France, for a time "forbidden on public streets because of bloodthirstiness."

Picture: Three-year-old male, dark brindle with white.

French Bulldog

A French companion dog with a charm all its own. Courageous and always eager to be very close to its people.

Height, weight: Up to 12 inches (30 cm); up to 26 pounds (12 kg). Thick-set and strong.
Coat and color: Short, dense, and shiny. From white to black; also brindle.
Appearance: Serious and menacing, but "laughs" with its body. Unmistakable.
Suitable for: People who would like a mastiff-type dog in a handier format.
Not suitable for: Someone living several flights up in a building without elevator.
Requirements: Adapts to any way of life.
Grooming: Not much needed.
Qualities as a family member: Very devoted; intuitively understands any mood. Undaunted, courageous, and effective watchdog that doesn't bark unnecessarily.
Breed character: A cheerful and amusing dog but not without dignity. Has a definite personality of its own and is not too ready to subordinate itself.
Problems associated with breed: Sensitive to heat and breathes noisily. Reluctant to mate; tends to have complicated births. Cannot therefore be raised in great numbers.
Ailments associated with breed: Abnormalities of the spinal column without disabling consequences. Also herniated disks.
Life expectancy: Medium.
Daily caloric needs: For a dog weighing 22 pounds (10 kg), 740 calories.
Remarks: Created around 1880 in France by crossing English bulldogs with terriers and pugs.
Picture: Piebald male, two years old.

Pug

The smallest of the mastiffs, this is a sturdy, well-proportioned toy breed of distinctive appearance.

Height, weight: Up to 12½ inches (32 cm); up to 17½ pounds (8 kg).
Coat and color: Short, glossy. Silver gray to apricot with black mask and dorsal stripe or "trace."
Appearance: A little sullen, with large, expressive eyes. Unmistakable.
Suitable for: Novices who want a quiet, uncomplicated dog that will thrive in a small apartment.
Not suitable for: Conventional people whose secret ideal is a German shepherd dog.
Requirements: Lots of love and not too much exercise.
Grooming: Not much needed.
Qualities as a family member: Pleasant because this dog is neither excitable nor dull. Not a yapper. Good watchdog. Very devoted.
Breed character: Pleasant and playful. A quiet, cheerful nature. Sometimes phlegmatic. Highly intelligent.
Problems associated with breed: Its breathing is highly audible. Easily becomes obese. Be sure to keep skin folds clean so eczema will not develop in them.
Ailments associated with breed: Danger of keratitis (inflammation of the cornea) and ulcers on the cornea. Catches colds easily. Otherwise robust.
Life expectancy: Up to 15 years.
Daily caloric needs: 600 calories.
Picture: Stone-gray bitch, four years old.

Basset Hound

This multicolored dog that three children can pet all at once always has its nose and ears to the ground. With its long, strong-boned body carried low on powerful paws and its sorrowful expression, this is not everyone's idea of a dog. But its fans love it. I've been living with bassets for a quarter of a century.

Height, weight: 13 to 14 inches (33–35.5 cm); heights over 15 inches (38 cm) at the highest point of the shoulder blades is a disqualification; about 66 pounds (30 kg). Should be strong and muscular.
Coat and color: Flat, short, and dense, not too fine. Tricolors: white, black, and red; white, black, and lemon; bicolor: white and red. But any hound colors are acceptable.
Appearance: Unmistakable and, for the layperson, confusing: a

giant dachshund. Unexpected but typical is its effortlessly smooth gait.
Suitable for: Strong people with good nerves and an appreciation for obstinate individuality.
Not suitable for: The average person, lovers of classical beauty, physically delicate or old people, fanatics of cleanliness, or anyone demanding absolute obedience.
Requirements: Needs to live in a normal-sized to large apartment and get at least a one-hour walk a day (in addition to going out to relieve itself). Since it has a pack mentality it doesn't like to be alone.
Grooming: Not much needed, but the eyes and ears have to be checked and cleaned regularly.
Qualities as a family member: Sociable. Not a watchdog, but can be quite noisy. Self-assured, with definite opinions and a will of its own.
Breed character: A

surprising mixture of laziness and liveliness. Mentally stable and robust almost to the point of insensitivity. Friendly at heart. But some males as well as bitches can be extremely dominant. Can easily be kept together with a second dog.
Problems associated with breed: Hard to train; can be very stubborn. Its booming voice is heard wide and far. Once it has picked up a scent it is almost impossible to control on the leash. In some lines, males have a congenital tendency to kidney stones. Females sometimes develop false pregnancy with considerable milk production. Males often display hypersexuality. A gap between the eyeball and the lower lid is unfortunately still listed as a desirable trait in the standard ("The red lining of the lower lid is visible.") In spite of its long back (it looks longer than it really is because the legs are so

short), there are no problems with slipped disks.
Life expectancy: About 12 years.
Daily caloric needs: For a 66-pound (30 kg) dog, about 1,700 calories.
Remarks: Basically a hunting dog that works in packs. One of the best tracking dogs even in the most difficult terrain. More persistent than almost any other dog, it can move with surprising agility. The push of its hind legs is impressive. The breed has survived its period of fashionableness without ill effects; in the 1970s, at the height of its popularity, there were a number of excitable basset hounds.
Picture: Three-year-old male.

Briard

Pyrenean Sheep dog

This herding dog that has become an ideal family dog is sometimes referred to in its French homeland as "a heart with hair all around it."

Height, weight: Males up to 27 inches (68 cm) at the withers; bitches 22 to 25½ inches (56–65 cm) at the withers; up to 66 pounds (30 kg). Muscular and well-proportioned.
Coat and color: Dense, long, "should squeak in your hand." All clear colors except white; dark colors preferred.
Appearance: Attracts attention with its "goat hair" and bushy eyebrows.
Suitable for: People who know something about dogs, can empathize with them, and have a firm hand.
Not suitable for: Anyone else, especially beginners or people who like to take it easy.
Requirements: Should not be kept outdoors but is not an apartment dog

either. Needs to be kept fairly busy.
Grooming: Regular brushing and combing. An occasional bath.
Qualities as a family member: Physically hardy with a tender soul. Loves its people beyond all else. Hates to be left alone. Good with children.
Breed character: Lively, quick, and intelligent. Full of fire.
Problems associated with breed: If not kept busy enough, it will find things to do on its own which don't always meet with the owner's approval. Loves rainy weather and brings dirt into the house.
Ailments associated with breed: Very healthy. Free of hip dysplasia and neurotic disorders. No susceptibilities described.
Life expectancy: High.
Daily caloric needs: For a dog weighing 66 pounds (30 kg), 1,700 calories.
Picture: Fauve bitch, four years old.

Not especially large or heavy, this dog is still one of the most energetic of the herding dogs.

(Recognized by the FCI)
Height, weight: From 15 to 19 inches (38–48 cm); 18 to 26 pounds (8–12 kg). The short-haired strain somewhat larger.
Coat and color: A mixture of goat hair and sheep's wool. Always thick, whether long or semi-long, and wind-blown. All colors except white permitted.
Appearance: Unique with its cunning, alert, and intelligent facial expression.
Suitable for: Very firm, consistent people who want a dog that is quiet indoors and full of vim and vigor on walks.
Not suitable for: People who are indecisive.
Requirements: Needs a lot of exercise. Can live outdoors.
Grooming: Not complicated.

Qualities as a family member: Very lively, and watchful, tough and hardy; defends all property. Suspicious of strangers; devoted to and very fond of children.
Breed character: A healthy dose of aggressiveness and a quick temper. Self-confident and independent. Females tend to be affectionate.
Problems associated with breed: Must not be trained to be aggressive or it will become very dangerous.
Ailments associated with breed: Very healthy.
Life expectancy: Lives to an old age.
Daily caloric needs: For a dog weighing 22 pounds (10 kg), 740 calories.
Remarks: Works not only as a herding dog but is also used for tracking and in avalanche rescue work.
Picture: On left, fauve male, two years old; on right, harlequin male, four years old.

Dachshund
Wirehaired, short-haired (or smooth), and long-haired

Of all dog breeds the dachshund is one of the best known. Even people who know almost nothing about dogs know its name and are aware of its amusing shape.

Height, weight: In dachshunds the circumference of the chest is measured. Normal dachshunds: From 14 to no more than 18 inches (35–45 cm); height at withers: up to 10½ inches (27 cm); 11 to 20 pounds (5–9 kg). Miniature or dwarf dachshunds: Up to 14 inches (35 cm) with corresponding height; 9 pounds (4 kg). Rabbit dachshunds: Up to 12 inches (30 cm); up to 8 pounds (3.5 kg).

Coat and color: Long-haired (the most popular strain; about 50 percent of all dachshunds): soft, sleek, silky, with feathering on tail. Solid red or two-colored black and brown. Wirehaired (second favorite;

40 percent): dense coat made up of wiry hairs distributed through wooly undercoat; beard and bushy eyebrows. All colors, but especially wild color. Short-haired (now relatively rare; only 10 percent): short, dense, and glossy. Solid red or bicolored black and brown.

Appearance: Well-proportioned, short-legged and long-bodied dogs, preferably robust-looking and with a bold and assertive carriage of the head.

Suitable for: City as well as country people with anything from a tiny to a huge apartment—in short, for anybody.

Not suitable for: People who find it hard to be firm and don't appreciate strength of character in dogs.

Requirements: Usually needs to be kept busy and get plenty of exercise, but sometimes just the opposite. The size of the living quarters is not

important, but if you live up on the third floor or higher there should be an elevator (see Ailments). Dachshunds are masters at not hearing you when you call them, but when trained for hunting they learn obedience.

Grooming: Regular combing and brushing for the long-haired strain. In general not much care required. Wirehaired dachshunds don't need to be trimmed or clipped.

Qualities as a family member: If trained with firmness, dachshunds are better behaved than their reputation would suggest. Capable of developing into a family tyrant. Good, though noisy watchdog.

Breed character: A robust, lively dog. Courageous, with a marked sense of self-esteem and a definite personality. Different temperaments to suit different requirements. Dogs from mass breeding operations (often the case with dachshunds) are

frequently timid or hysterical.

Problems associated with breed: Climbing and especially descending stairs is not good for dachshund puppies because it can lead to loose shoulder joints. Wrong training can turn a dachshund into a fighter that constantly challenges bigger dogs. There are pugnacious daredevils, especially among the wirehaired strain, that refuse to realize that they are no match for a boxer or a German shepherd dog.

Ailments associated with breed: "Dachshund paralysis" is a collective term for disorders that often affect dogs with long backs. Paralysis is caused by pinched nerves. The severity of the disorders ranges from rheumatism to herniated disks to ossifications of the spinal column. Dachshund paralysis first manifests itself in dogs four to five years old and

disappears for good if cured. That is why it's important to consult a veterinarian at the first sign of abnormal movement in the hindquarters. Early treatment is crucial. On the whole one can say that the stronger the build and the more normal the proportions between the length and height of an animal, the less you need to worry. Male dachshunds tend to get kidney stones, and the short-haired strain is subject to loss of hair due to mite infestation. Red long-haired dachshunds sometimes exhibit an unnatural urge to bite and attack (see cocker madness, page 150). Older, obese dachshunds may get diabetes.
Life expectancy: 12 to 14 years.
Daily caloric needs: For a dog weighing 16½ pounds (7.5 kg), about 600 calories.
Remarks: The "German dachshunds" mentioned

in hunting books of the sixteenth century and in Konrad Gessner's natural history (1551) are of the short-haired variety. The wirehaired dachshund is first mentioned in 1811 by Carl Emil Hartig, a writer on hunting. His remark that "...they are not usually as short-legged and crooked as the smooth-haired..." suggests that terriers were crossed in. Probably the breed used in the cross was the Scottish Dandie Dinmont terrier, a somewhat strange-looking terrier, robust and reminiscent of a dachsund, with a topknot of soft hair. Since this terrier often has a pepper and salt coat, the wirehaired dachshund's coloring comes from this source.
Long-haired dachshunds are documented only late in literature. In 1880, Carl Emil Diezel mentions a straight- and long-legged, long-haired dachshund as a useful hunter. He writes:

"Dachshunds are no doubt among the most charming of dogs. They are exceedingly loyal, affectionate, and complaisant and at the same time intelligent and easy to teach. Indoors they behave extremely well and are very clean. They make loyal, sharp, and reliable watchdogs for a farm, and for a hunter, the dachshund is an indispensable companion—in short, a universally adaptable dog."
The crooked legs as an ideal of dachsund beauty lasted only a short time, but they did succeed in lending the dachshund notoriety. Even humor magazines featured the breed, especially in cartoons. The first book to be written about dachshunds appeared in 1885 and is entitled *The Dachshund; Its History, Breeding, Training, and Uses*. Its author, R. Cornelli, suggests "Any hunter who has forest hunting privileges should

keep a pair of dachshunds."
Picture on page 160, left: Wirehaired male, wild color, six years old.
Picture on page 160, right: Short-haired bitch, black and red, two years old.
Picture above: Long-haired male, red with darker cover hair, two years old.

Basenji

Descended from an ancient Central African breed that was never crossed with any other breed. An elegant dog that attracts attention and doesn't bark.

Height, weight: Males 16 to 17 inches (40–43 cm) from the ground to the top of the shoulder; bitches 16 inches (40 cm); up to 26 pounds (12 kg).
Coat and color: Short and silky; stretchy skin. Fox-red, pure black, or black and tan; feet, chest, and tip of tail always white.
Appearance: Springy gait; small, pointed ears; ringtail carried high. An exotic dog.
Suitable for: People with a sense for the out of the ordinary and an appreciation for a sweet, unusual, and clean dog.
Not suitable for: People who don't like to call attention to themselves.
Requirements: Happiest if two or three are kept together; they will not fight among themselves. Needs space and exercise.
Grooming: Not much needed.
Qualities as a family member: If the apartment is large enough, an ideal apartment dog: doesn't smell, is clean as a cat. Doesn't bark, yodels instead. Very affectionate and cheerful.
Breed character: Very attentive pack hunting dog of the African continent; gregarious. Highly intelligent and affectionate.
Problems associated with breed: Very clever at getting its way. Succeeds less by obstinacy than by charm.
Ailments associated with breed: Anemic by nature, but can be cured.
Life expectancy: About 12 years.
Daily caloric needs: For a dog weighing 22 pounds (10 kg), 740 calories.
Picture: Red and white bitch, 1½ years old.

Shih Tzu

The famous "lion" dog of ancient China, which actually originated in Tibet, has now become very popular in the West.

The name Shih Tzu means "lion." The breed, which originated in Tibet, has found a new home in the United States, where it is very popular.
Height, weight: Up to 10½ inches (27 cm); from 9 to 15 pounds (4–7 kg). Longer than tall.
Coat and color: Long and thick, with undercoat. The hair looks rougher than it is. A beard and moustache reinforce the general impression of hairiness. All colors permitted, but a white mark on the forehead is desirable.
Appearance: A markedly arrogant air.
Suitable for: People who appreciate the exotic and are looking for a small "big" dog.
Not suitable for: People with little time and with neighbors who object to noise.
Requirements: Wants to be kept busy; doesn't need much space.
Grooming: Time-consuming daily coat care.
Qualities as a family member: Adopts one person as its leader. Needs lots of love and is fond of children.
Breed character: Moderate need for exercise. Loves to play. Is as robust as a working dog. Very watchful.
Problems associated with breed: Brings a lot of dirt into the house during bad weather.
Ailments associated with breed: Excellent health except for a tendency to eye abnormalities.
Life expectancy: Very high: 15 years or more.
Daily caloric needs: 530 calories.
Picture: Right, a 16-month old gold and white bitch; left, a four-year old gold and white male.

West Highland White Terrier

A small hunting breed from Scotland, robust, strong, and still healthy. In danger of being made into a lapdog by present fashion.

Height, weight: 11 inches (28 cm); 18 to 22 pounds (8–10 kg). Compact body.

Coat and color: Wirehaired; outer coat of hard hair and an under-coat that is thick, short, soft, and close. Pure white without any yellow tinge.

Appearance: A cute, dainty head with a muzzle that is not too long. Short ears.

Suitable for: People who feel affection for a lovable little "big" dog, have plenty of time, and are willing to devote it to the dog.

Not suitable for: People who follow fads and want a cute-looking little dog to show off.

Requirements: Needs sufficient exercise and lots of love, but also firm discipline. Its tempera-ment can be kept in line only if it is kept occupied and even given real "work" to do. Very willing to learn and perform tricks. But first has to have a chance every day to romp to its heart's content.

Grooming: Thorough brushing and combing every day; trimming every three months. Shouldn't look too styled.

Qualities as a family member: A cheerful dog for children; a real companion. Doesn't yap. Makes a good watchdog with surprisingly strong teeth.

Breed character: Extremely self-assured toward other dogs; robust. Doesn't pick fights. Has disarming charm.

Problems associated with breed: Because of its unrestrained hunting instinct it has to be kept on a leash in the countryside. If it is not given a chance to work off its excess energy by romping, it may become aggressive.

Ailments associated with breed: Watch out with puppies from pet stores or kennels specializing in fashionable breeds: They may develop hip problems while still young (Perthe's disease) or get itches and skin irritations as allergic reactions.

Life expectancy: Gets quite old.

Daily caloric needs: Depending on weight from 597 to 790 calories.

Remarks: The Westie is the white dog in the ad for Black and White whiskey. The black dog is a Scottish terrier. Lord Buchanan had both dogs painted in 1892.

The breed goes back to the middle of the last century, when Scottish hunters wanted a white hunting dog so that it would not be mistaken for game. Westies were very fashionable around 1927. A magazine wrote: "There has been a palace revolution, and His Canine Majesty, the Pekinese, has had to abdicate in favor of the intelligent West Highland White."

Picture: Male, four years old.

Yorkshire Terrier

The layperson is tempted to ask: Is it a toy or a dog? The answer is clearly "dog." This tiny dog with its fancy coat has much going for it. In earlier days it was the "pocket weapon" of poachers.

Height, weight: 8 to 9½ inches (20–24 cm); up to 7 pounds (3.2 kg). Less than 4½ pounds (2 kg) is not acceptable according to the standard. Dainty, compact, and well-proportioned.

Coat and color: The silky hair—without undercoat—is long, straight, and smooth. It lies on the body like a coat. Dark steel blue from the back of the head to the base of the tail; head, chest, and legs, tan with the darkest shade on the ears.

Appearance: What is most striking is the long hair parted along the midline and hanging down straight on both sides from the nose to the end of the tail.

Suitable for: People in tiny apartments who want a dog that is appropriately small but still a dog. They also have to be willing to spend the time necessary to keep the dog's coat groomed.

Not suitable for: Someone who wants to give a dog a friendly smack now and then or who doesn't like carrying a dog.

Requirements: Doesn't need much exercise because it keeps in motion wherever it is; should nevertheless have a daily walk.

Grooming: Brush, comb, and lightly oil every day; bathe once a month. Hair has to be trimmed on ears and paws every six weeks. Keep the long hair on the head out of the dog's face by pinning it up or tying it with a ribbon to keep it from bothering the dog's eyes and drooping into the food dish at mealtimes.

Qualities as a family member: Charming and watchful, but can be a yapper. Cuddly and very playful, so that even children enjoy the dog.

Breed character: Lively and fearless. Not a timid miniature. Isn't afraid of larger dogs. Defends its own things and its owner's property.

Problems associated with breed: Has been indiscriminately bred because it is a fashionable breed. Therefore often corresponds to the breed standard only externally and is overpriced. Good Yorkies that live up to the type should therefore be purchased only from conscientious breeders.

Ailments associated with breed: Paralysis in the hindquarters caused by herniated disks and other problems of the spine. Abnormal skull formations in Yorkies measuring less than 8 inches (20 cm). These pocket-sized dogs range from nervous to neurotic.

Life expectancy: High, up to 14 years.

Daily caloric needs: For a dog weighing 6½ pounds (3 kg), 315 calories.

Remarks: Bred in the nineteenth century in the Duchy of York as a hunting dog that could penetrate into badger and fox burrows. When its hair grew longer, breeders made it into a fashion dog and tried to reduce its size. The same is happening today. That is why the measurements in the standard should be strictly observed. Officially there is no such thing as a mini-Yorkshire.

Picture: In front, bitch; in back, male.

Tibetan Terrier
Tibetan Apso

Pekinese

A Tibetan breed that is covered all over with hair (the meaning of the word "apso"). A very lovable dog.

Height, weight: 13 to 16 inches (34–40 cm); 18 to 31 pounds (8–14 kg). Compact and sturdy.
Coat and color: Double coat; with fine, long top coat, straight or slightly wavy. The hair on the forehead droops over the eyes. White; gold; sand, or smoke gray; black; also two- and three-colored.
Appearance: Reminiscent of a tiny Old English sheepdog.
Suitable for: People looking for a small, different-looking, uncomplicated dog.
Not suitable for: Fanatics about cleanliness who are upset by the slightest bit of dust.
Requirements: Uncomplicated; needs regular but not very extensive walks.
Grooming: Time-consuming coat care; comb again and again. None of the hair should be trimmed.
Qualities as a family member: Cheerful, affectionate, intelligent, and very devoted to its people.
Breed character: Good watchdog, wary of strangers. If there is occasion, will attack without hesitation, but is not a fighter.
Problems associated with breed: Must be trained not to resist being combed and bathed.
Ailments associated with breed: Not susceptible to illness. Except for some reproductive problems (lack of semen), nothing is mentioned in the literature.
Life expectancy: 16 years and more.
Daily caloric needs: For a dog weighing 22 pounds (10 kg), 740 calories.
Picture: At left, black and white male; at right, bitch, gold.

From the imperial palace of China, this is a noble, exotic dog with a curiously "rolling" gait.

Height, weight: 6 to 10 inches (15–25 cm); 3½ to 13 pounds (1.5-6 kg). Strong-boned, body close to the ground.
Coat and color: Double coat with thick undercoat and long, straight topcoat. Carries a mane. All colors permitted.
Appearance: Very exotic with its pushed-in face and amazing long hair.
Suitable for: People without children but with an appreciation for the unusual.
Not suitable for: Families with lots of children or people who want "just a plain normal dog."
Requirements: Anything from a small apartment on up. Needs disciplined training and no pampering.
Grooming: Frequent combing and brushing, regular cleaning of the wrinkles in the face.
Qualities as a family member: Watchfulness manifested in barking. Easily develops into a family tyrant.
Breed character: Self-assured and fearless. A daredevil with a strong will of its own. Loving to the point of jealousy.
Problems associated with breed: Has sensitive eyes and catches colds easily. Not a dog for children.
Ailments associated with breed: Very difficult births. Herniated disks and dislocated kneecaps. Trichiasis (lashes growing inward toward the eyeball).
Life expectancy: With healthy dogs, 16 to 18 years.
Daily caloric needs: For a dog weighing 8 pounds (3.5 kg), 360 calories.
Picture: At left, male, light red brindle, one year old; at right, black male, six years old.

Chihuahua

Miniature Pinscher

This tiny dog is named after a Mexican town at the foot of the Sierra Madre.

Height, weight: Never over 8 inches (20 cm); from 1 to 5½ pounds (.5–2.5 kg). Lively and graceful.
Coat and color: Short, thick, and shiny or long and soft. All colors, solid, marked, or splashed.
Appearance: A miniature dog with bat ears. The smallest of all breeds.
Suitable for: People who would like a really small lapdog.
Not suitable for: People who don't like small things.
Requirements: Adapts to its owner, on whose arm it feels happiest.
Grooming: The long-haired strain needs regular brushing; otherwise little care required. Keep eyes clean.
Qualities as a family member: Very attached; hardly barks at all but has a kind of mutter with which it announces anything strange. Highly intelligent.
Breed character: Hardy and courageous. Loves to romp. Very lively; not a dog for children.
Problems associated with breed: Should not be pampered by being kept indoors all the time (relieving itself on the balcony) and being carried around constantly.
Ailments associated with breed: Almost immune to the usual diseases affecting puppies. The short-haired strain may lose its hair. Birth complications and dental problems.
Life expectancy: High.
Daily caloric needs: For a dog weighing 3½ pounds (1.5 kg), 190 calories.
Picture: Long-haired variety; on left, male, apricot with white, six years old; on right, male, black and tan, six years old.

A very spirited toy dog that is a "big" dog in pocket size. Robust in spite of its fragile appearance.

Height, weight: 11 to 11½ inches (28-29 cm) at the withers; a dog of either sex measuring under 10 inches (25½ cm) or over 12½ inches (32 cm) shall be disqualified; 7 to 9 pounds (3–4 kg). A miniature version of the Doberman pinscher.
Coat and color: Short, thick, shiny, and close to the body. Solid brown in various shades to fawn or two-colored black with red or brown markings.
Appearance: Small, but in no sense dwarflike.
Suitable for: People in small apartments who would like a real dog.
Not suitable for: Anyone with noise-sensitive neighbors.
Requirements: Not a dog to be carried in your arms or handbag but one that catches mice and likes going for walks.
Grooming: Not much needed.
Qualities as a family member: Watchful; unfortunately yaps more than just now and then. Affectionate. Charming, enjoys playing little tricks, and is totally devoted to its people.
Breed character: Lively temperament, very intuitive. Doesn't mind being alone occasionally.
Problems associated with breed: Dogs that have been bred smaller than the prescribed standard lose all their endearing qualities.
Ailments associated with breed: Robust dog that hardly ever gets sick. Tendency to develop kidney stones and hip problems.
Life expectancy: Very high.
Daily caloric needs: 360 calories.
Picture: At left, red bitch, two years old; at right, black and red bitch, 2½ years old.

Addresses and Literature

For Information and Printed Materials:

American Boarding Kennel Association
4575 Galley Road, Suite 400A
Colorado Springs, Colorado 80915
(Publishes lists of approved kennels.)

American Society for the Prevention of Cruelty to
Animals (ASPCA)
441 East 92nd Street
New York, New York 10028

American Veterinary Medical Association
930 North Meacham Road
Schaumburg, Illinios 60173

Gaines TWT
P.O. Box 8172
Kankakee, Illinios 60901
(Publishes "Touring with Towser," a directory of hotels
and motels that accommodate guests with dogs.)

Humane Society of the Unted States
2100 L Street N.W.
Washington, DC 20037

International Kennel Clubs:

The American Kennel Club (AKC)
51 Madison Avenue
New York, New York 10038

Australian National Kennel Club
Royal Show Grounds
Ascot Vale
Victoria
Australia

Canadian Kennel Clubs
111 Eglington Avenue
Toronto 12, Ontario
Canada

Irish Kennel Club
41 Harcourt Street
Dublin, 2
Ireland

The Kennel Club
1–4 Clargis Street Picadilly
London W7Y 8AB
England

New Zealand Kennel Club
P.O. Box 523
Wellington, 1
New Zealand

*Double spread on
following pages: Brown
Newfoundland.*

BIBLIOGRAPHY

Alderton, David, *The Dog Care Manual*, Barron's Educational Series, Inc., Hauppauge, New York, 1986.

Antesberger, H., *The German Shepherd Dog*, Barron's Educational Series, Inc., Hauppauge, New York, 1985.

Atkinson, James, *Chow Chows*, Barron's Educational Series, Inc., Hauppauge, New York, 1988.

Fiedelmeier, Leni, *Dachshunds*, Barron's Educational Series, Inc., Hauppauge, New York, 1984.

Frye, Fredric L., *First Aid For Your Dog*, Barron's Educational Series, Inc., Hauppauge, New York, 1987.
————,*Mutts*, Barron's Educational Series, Inc., Hauppauge, New York, 1989.
————,*Schnauzers*, Barron's Educational Series, Inc., Hauppauge, New York 1988.

Gudas, Raymond, *Doberman Pinschers*, Barron's Educational Series, Inc., Hauppauge, New York, 1987.

Kern, Kerry, *Labrador Retrievers*, Barron's Educational Series, Inc., Hauppauge, New York, 1987.

————,*The Terrier Handbook*, Barron's Educational Series, Inc., Hauppauge, New York, 1988.

Kraupa-Tuskany, H.F., *Boxers*, Barron's Educational Series, Inc., Hauppauge, New York, 1988.

Lorenz, Konrad Z. *Man Meets Dog*. Penguin Books, London and New York, 1967.

Smythe, Reginald H. *The Mind of the Dog*. Thomas, Bannerstone House, London, 1961.

Sucher, Jamie J., *Golden Retrievers*, Barron's Educational Series, Inc., Hauppauge, New York, 1987.

Ullmann, H.J., *The Dog Handbook*, Barron's Educational Series, Inc., Hauppauge, New York, 1984.
————,and E. Ullmann, *Poodles*, Barron's Educational Series, Hauppauge, New York, 1984.
————,*Spaniels*, Barron's Educational Series, Inc., Hauppauge, New York, 1982.

Vriends-Parent, Lucia, *Beagles*, Barron's Educational Series, Inc., Hauppauge, New York, 1987.

INDEX

Important Notes

This pet owner's guide tells the reader how to buy and care for a dog. The author and the publisher consider it important to point out that the advice given in the book is meant primarily for normally developed puppies from a good breeder—that is, dogs of excellent physical health and good character.

Anyone who adopts a fully grown dog should be aware that the animal has already formed its basic impressions of human beings. The new owner should watch the animal carefully, including its behavior toward humans, and should meet the previous owner. If the dog comes from a shelter, it may be possible to get some information on the dog's background and peculiarities there. There are dogs that as a result of bad experiences with humans behave in an unnatural manner or may even bite. Only people who have experience with dogs should take in such an animal.

Even well-behaved and carefully supervised dogs sometimes do damage to someone else's property or cause accidents. It is therefore in the owner's interest to be adequately insured against such eventualities, and we strongly urge all dog owners to purchase a liability policy that covers their dog.

Acknowledgments

The author and the publisher would like to thank the photographer, Monika Wegler, for her enthusiastic cooperation. Thanks to her years of experience with dogs and with dog owners and with the help of the most modern photographic techniques, Ms. Wegler has succeeded in taking extraordinarily natural and expressive pictures of dogs. Among them are portraits of prizewinning pedigree dogs, unusual mongrels, and cute puppies.

The photographer and the publisher want to thank all dog owners, breeders, and veterinarians, as well as dog clubs and associations for their cooperation.

About the Author

Ulrich Klever was born in 1922 and lives with his family and two basset hounds on a farm in Bavaria. He is the most successful writer on dogs in Germany. Mr. Klever has written eight books on dogs that have earned him international acclaim.

All inquiries should be addressed to:
Barron's Educational Series, Inc.
250 Wireless Boulevard
Hauppauge, NY 11788

Library of Congress Catalog Card No. 89-6796

International Standard Book No. 0-8120-4158-5

Library of Congress Cataloging-in-Publication Data

Klever, Ulrich, 1922-
    [Hunde. English]
    The complete book of dog care : an expert's advice on how to raise a happy and healthy dog / Ulrich Klever; with 180 photographs by Monika Wegler; consulting editor, Matthew M. Vriends.
        Translation of: Hunde.
        Includes index.
        ISBN 0-8120-4158-5
        1. Dogs. I. Title
SF427.K4513   1989
636.7—dc20   89-6796

PRINTED IN HONG KONG
456   4900   98

Photos on back cover
upper row: Chihuahua, wirehaired dachshund, Akita;
middle row: miniature poodle, Airedale terrier, Old English Sheepdogs;
lower row: kuvasz, Afghan hound, German shepherd dog.

CAN YOU IDENTIFY THESE PUPPIES?

Page 152, right

Page 148, right

Page 163

Page 161

Page 131, left

Page 153

Page 132

Page 158

Page 157, right